Church Denominations and their Beliefs

By Larry J Tate

Copyright © 2022 by Larry J Tate

ISBN: 9798422481453

Bible Translations

All scripture quotations are taken from the *Holy Bible*, King James Version, Cambridge, 1769. Used by permission. All rights reserved.

Table of Contents

Introduction

We've all had that knock on the door, and staring us in the face is someone handing out tracts, wanting to invite us to church, and perhaps even, wanting to talk about Church doctrine. Wouldn't it be nice to know what they believe before entering into a conversation with them? Even better, wouldn't it be convenient for us to be able to witness right back at them, using Scriptural references to back up our own beliefs?

We've all wondered from time-to-time, "What exactly, do other churches believe? Where did they come from? What are their roots?" How have they evolved over time? It would take an entire library to fully understand every church and their beliefs, but this book will provide the basics of various church organizations, and their beliefs.

Before delving into the myriad of Christian churches and beliefs however, it is first necessary to speak not only of the beginnings of Christianity, but Judaism as well. Judaism is the world's oldest monotheistic religion. Followers of Judaism believe in the one-true God who revealed himself by way of ancient prophets. Through Moses, God revealed his Law and the Ten Commandments, and then came the Written Torah, also known as the Pentateuch, or the Five Books of Moses, namely Genesis, Exodus, Leviticus, Numbers, and Deuteronomy. Finally, the Hebrew Bible contains other books on the subject of history, prophecy, wisdom and poetry.

Out of Judaism sprang Christianity, hence the term, "Judeo-Christian," which is used to link Christianity and Judaism together. This is due to the fact that Christianity had its beginnings among the Jews, and Christians worldwide continue to base their beliefs on the Jewish Scripture of the Old Testament, as well as the New Testament.

The term, "Christian" was coined in the New Testament. *"And when he had found him, he brought him unto Antioch. And it came to pass, that a whole year they assembled themselves with the church, and taught much people. And the disciples were called Christians first in Antioch."* (Acts 11:26)

It was through Jewish Christians that Christianity began to spread throughout the Gentile World. Over time however, most of the Jewish population reverted back to traditional Judaism, and as a general rule, they have disavowed any connection to

Christianity. Now, Christianity thrives among non-Jewish peoples around the world.

Catholic

Overview. New Testament Christianity spread from Jerusalem to Asia and Europe. At that time, it was known as the "katholikos," or the "Universal Church, a term coined by Ignatius of Antioch in his letter to the Smyrnaeans in approximately 105 to 110 A.D. He is believed to have known the Apostle John directly, and is best known for his seven epistles which were written to the Ephesians, Magnesians, Trallians, Romans, Philadelphians, Smyrnaeans, and Polycarp. In his letter to the Smyrnaeans, he said, *"Wherever the bishop appears, there let the multitude be; even as wherever Christ Jesus is, there is the catholic (katholikos) Church."*[1] This was only about ten years or less after the Apostle John died. The terms, "catholic," or "universal," was simply a way of describing the one and only early Church, and were utilized centuries before the Roman Catholic Church was formally organized. Still today, in God's eyes, there is but one universal Church.[2]

It was in Rome where the Roman Catholic Church would eventually find its beginnings. At first, it was simply one of the many churches founded by New Testament Apostles, but over a period of many years, the Church at Rome became more and more organized. There is great deal of argument as to when the Church at Rome officially became the Roman Catholic Church. Today's Catholic Church insists that the Apostle Peter was its first Pope. However, most historians disagree with that statement, and say it was centuries later before the Catholic Church became an organization of its own. Some claim the Catholic Church had its official beginning with Emperor Theodosius when he issued his Edict of Thessalonica in 380 A.D., where he said, *"We order the followers of this law to embrace the name of Catholic Christians."* On the other hand, some historians tell us the Catholic Church had its beginning with Roman Bishop Leo I (440-461 A.D.), who was the first to claim full, supreme, and universal power over the whole Church. Still others believe the Roman Catholic Church officially became an institution when Gregory I was appointed as Bishop of Rome in 590 A.D. and introduced liturgical reforms that are still maintained by today's Catholic Church.

In the beginning, the Church at Rome believed and operated entirely on the basis of the Apostles' Doctrine. As time went on however, the beliefs and doctrines of the Church began to evolve. The most prominent evolution of beliefs had to do with the Doctrine of the Trinity.

The Nicene and subsequent Creeds. The fourth century opened up, not with an agreement about the Godhead, but with a great deal of controversy, primarily involving a conflict between the doctrines of Athanasius and Arius. While Arius agreed with some of the Oneness/Monarchian beliefs of Sabellius, he went much further, proclaiming Christ to be a created being, not of the same essence as the Father, and not co-equal with the Father.

Fearing disunity would lead to trouble for the Roman Empire, Constantine called the Council of Nicaea hoping to determine binding interpretations of Church doctrine. Attending the Council of Nicaea, was one group who favored Arianism, and another group favoring the doctrine in Athanasius. By the time the council came to an end, they finally adopted a creed that some regard as a quasi-

Oneness/Monarchian doctrine of God, but at the same time, denouncing Arianism.

While setting the stage for stronger Trinitarian language in later creeds, this first creed fell a bit short, simply stating that Christ was of the same essence (the Greek word "*homoousios*") as the Father and not just a similar essence (the Greek word "homoiousios") preferred by the Arians. The original doctrinal statement formulated by the Council of Nicaea in relation to the Godhead read, *"We believe in one God, the Father Almighty, maker of all things visible and invisible. And in one Lord Jesus Christ, the Son of God, begotten of the Father the only-begotten; that is, of the essence of the Father, God of God, Light of Light, very God of very God, begotten, not made, being of one substance (ὁμοούσιον, or homoousios) with the Father; by whom all things were made both in heaven and on earth; who for us men, and for our salvation, came down and was incarnate and was made man; he suffered, and the third day he rose again, ascended into heaven; from thence he shall come to judge the quick and the dead. And in the Holy Ghost. But those who say: 'There was a time when he was not;' and 'He was not before he was made;' and 'He was made out of nothing,' or 'He is of another substance' or 'essence,' or 'The Son of God is created,' or 'changeable,' or 'alterable'—they are condemned by the holy catholic (universal) and apostolic Church.* "[3]

As a result of the agreements made at the Council of Nicaea, Constantine issued an edict against Arius, and he was deposed from his official position in the Church. The edict read, *"The great and victorious Constantine Augustus to the bishops and laity: Since Arius is an imitator of the wicked and the ungodly, it is only right that he should suffer the same dishonor as they. Porphyry, who was hostile to anyone who feared God, composed a book which transgressed against our religion, and has found a suitable reward: namely that he has been disgraced from that time onward, his reputation is completely terrible, and his ungodly writings have been destroyed. In the same way it seems appropriate that Arius and those of like mind with Arius should from now on be called Porphyrians, so that their name is taken from those whose ways they have imitated. In addition, if any writing composed by Arius should be found, it should be handed over to the flames, so that not only will the wickedness of his teaching be obliterated, but nothing will be left even to remind anyone of him. And I hereby make a public order, that if someone should be discovered to have hidden a writing composed by Arius, and not to have immediately brought it forward and destroyed it by fire, his penalty shall be death. As soon as he is discovered in this offense, he shall be submitted for capital punishment.*"[4]

It didn't take long however, for Constantine to gradually became more lenient toward Arius whom he had recently exiled. Though he never disavowed the Council of Nicaea or its decrees, the emperor ultimately permitted Arius to return home after he agreed not to be so vocal with his theological ideas. Then, in 335 A.D., Constantine called the Council of Jerusalem with the intention of officially re-admitting Arius and his followers back into the Church. By the end of the council, the attending members finally came to an agreement, and issued a letter allowing Arius back in fellowship with the Church. The letter read, *"The Holy Council assembled in Jerusalem by the grace of God, etc.….their orthodox teaching in writing, which we all confessed to be sound and ecclesiastical. And he reasonably recommended that they should be received and united to the Church of God, as you will know yourselves from the transcript of the same Epistle, which we have transmitted to your reverences. We believe that yourselves also, as if recovering the very members of your own body, will experience great joy and gladness, in acknowledging and recovering your own bowels, your own brethren and fathers; since not only the Presbyters, Arius and his fellows, are given back to you, but also the whole Christian people and the entire multitude, which on occasion of the aforesaid men have a long time been in dissension among you. Moreover it were fitting, now that you know for certain what has passed, and that the men have communicated with us and have been received by so great a Holy Council, that you should with all readiness hail this your coalition and peace with your own members, specially since the articles of the faith which they have published preserve indisputable the universally confessed apostolical tradition and teaching.* "[5]

With the Arians back in fellowship, and Constantine nearing the end of his life, he asked Arian Bishop Eusebius of Nicomedia to baptize him on his deathbed in 337 A.D. After Constantine's death, his son Constantius II succeeded him as emperor. Constantius was an Arian sympathizer, and under his power, Arianism rose to its highest point at the Third Council of Sirmium in 357 A.D. The Seventh Arian Confession, also known as the Second Sirmium Confession held that both "homoousios" (of one substance) and "homoiousios" (of similar substance) were unbiblical and that the Father is greater than the Son, all but overturning the Nicene Creed of 325 A.D. The Second Sirmium Confession read, *"It is held for certain that there is one God, the Father Almighty, as also is preached in all the world. And His one only-begotten Son, our Lord Jesus Christ, generated from Him before the ages; and that we may not speak of two Gods, since the Lord Himself has said, 'I go to my Father and your Father, and my God and your God' (John 20:17). On this account He is God of all, as also the Apostle taught: 'Is He God of the Jews only, is He not also of the Gentiles? Yes of the Gentiles also; since there is one God who shall justify the circumcision from faith, and the uncircumcision through faith' (Romans 3:29, 30). And everything else agrees, and has no ambiguity. But since many persons are disturbed by questions concerning what is called in Latin substantia, but in Greek ousia, that is, to make it understood more exactly, as to 'coessential,' or what is called, 'like-in-essence,' there ought to be no mention of any of these at all, nor exposition of them in the Church, for this reason and for this consideration, that in divine Scripture nothing is written about them, and that they are above men's knowledge and above men's understanding; and because no one can declare the Son's generation, as it is written, 'Who shall declare His generation?' (Isaiah 53:8) For it is plain that the Father only knows how He generated the Son, and again the Son how He has been generated by the Father. And to none can it be a question that the Father is greater. For no one can doubt that the Father is greater in honor and dignity and Godhead, and in the very name of Father, the Son Himself testifying, 'The Father that sent me is greater than I' (John 10:29, 14:28) And no one is ignorant, that it is catholic doctrine, that there are two persons of Father and Son, and that the Father is greater, and the Son subordinated to the Father together with all things which the Father has subordinated to Him, and that the Father has no beginning, and is invisible, and immortal, and impassible; but that the Son has been generated from the Father, God from God, light from light, and that His origin, as aforesaid, no one knows, but the Father only. And that the Son Himself and our Lord and God, took flesh, that is, a body, that is, man, from Mary the virgin, as the Angel preached beforehand; and as all the Scriptures teach, and especially the apostle himself, the doctor of the Gentiles, Christ took man of Mary the virgin, through which he has suffered. And the whole faith is summed up, and secured in this, that a Trinity should ever be preserved, as we read in the Gospel, 'Go and baptize all the nations in the name of the Father and of the*

Son and of the Holy Ghost' (Matthew 28:19). And entire and perfect is the number of the Trinity; but the Paraclete, the Holy Ghost, sent forth through the Son, came according to the promise, that He might teach and sanctify the Apostles and all believers."[6]

Debates over the Godhead continued throughout the coming years, sometimes with Arianism coming out on top, and other times with Trinitarian beliefs as the victor. Then in 360 A.D., at the Council of Constantinople, a compromise was reached, allowing for both views to be accepted. The resulting creed read, *"We believe in one God, Father Almighty, from whom are all things. And in the only-begotten Son of God, begotten from God before all ages and before every beginning, by whom all things were made, visible and invisible, and begotten as only-begotten, only from the Father only, God from God, like to the Father that begat Him according to the Scriptures; whose origin no one knows, except the Father alone who begat Him. He as we acknowledge the only-begotten Son of God, the Father having sent Him, came here from the heavens, as it is written, for the undoing of sin and death, and was born of the Holy Ghost, of Mary the virgin according to the flesh, as it is written, and conversed with the disciples, and having fulfilled the whole*

Economy according to the Father's will, was crucified and died and was buried and ascended to the parts below the earth, at whom hades itself shuddered; who also rose from the dead on the third day, and abode with the disciples, and forty days being fulfilled, was taken up into the heavens, and sits on the right hand of the Father to come in the last day of the resurrection in the Father's glory, that He may render to every man according to his works. And in the Holy Ghost, whom the only-begotten Son of God Himself, Christ, our Lord and God, promised to send to the race of man, as Paraclete, as it is written, 'the Spirit of truth' (John 16:13), which He sent to the them when He had ascended into the heavens. But the name of 'essence,' which was set down by the Fathers in simplicity, and, being unknown by the people, caused offense, because the Scriptures do not contain it, it has seemed good to abolish, and for the future to make no mention of it at all; since the divine scriptures have made no mention of the essence of Father and Son. For neither ought 'subsistence' to be named concerning Father, Son and Holy Ghost. But we say that the Son is like the Father, as the divine Scriptures say and teach; and all the heresies, both those which have been already condemned, and whatever are of modern date, being contrary to this published statement, be they anathema."[7]

In 380 A.D., Emperor Theodosius, who reigned from 379-395 A.D., issued the Edict of Thessalonica, which established Christianity as the official State Religion. The Edict of Thessalonica read, *"It is our desire that all the various nations which are subject to our Clemency and Moderation, should continue to profess that religion which was delivered to the Romans by the divine Apostle Peter, as it has been preserved by faithful tradition, and which is now professed by the Pontiff Damasus and by Peter, Bishop of Alexandria, a man of apostolic holiness. According to the apostolic teaching and the doctrine of the Gospel, let us believe in the one deity of the Father and of the Son and of the Holy Spirit, in equal majesty and in a holy Trinity. We order the followers of this law to embrace the name of Catholic Christians; but as for the others, since, in our judgment they are foolish madmen, we decree that they shall be branded with the ignominious name of heretics, and shall not presume to give to their conventicles the name of churches. They will suffer in the first place the chastisement of the divine condemnation and in the second the punishment of our authority which in accordance with the will of Heaven we shall decide to inflict.* "[8]

Now that Christianity was the official State Religion, Emperor Theodosius went a step further to totally repress and remove Arianism from Christian thinking. He summoned a new council at Constantinople in 381 A.D. to re-affirm and expand the Nicene Creed of 325 A.D. This new creed settled another issue that had been rocking the Church after the Council of Nicaea, which was the relation of the Holy Spirit to God. What they wrestled with had to do with the question of whether the Holy Spirit was a distinct person in the Godhead, or not. By the time the council was over, they decided the Holy Spirit was a distinct person like the Father and the Son. Therefore, it is much more strongly Trinitarian than the original Nicene Creed of 325 A.D. The doctrinal statement formulated by the Council at Constantinople in 381 read, *"We believe in one God, the Father Almighty, Maker of heaven and earth, and of all things visible and invisible. We believe in one Lord Jesus Christ, the only-begotten Son of God, begotten of the Father before all worlds, Light of Light, very God of very God, begotten, not made, being of one substance with the Father; by whom all things were made; who for us men, and for our salvation, came down from heaven, and was incarnate by the Holy Ghost of the Virgin Mary, and was made man; he was crucified for us under Pontius Pilate, and suffered, and was buried, and the third day he rose again, according to the Scriptures, and ascended into heaven, and sitteth on the right hand of the Father; from thence he shall come again, with glory, to judge the quick and the dead; whose kingdom shall have no end. And in the Holy Ghost, the Lord and Giver of life, who proceedeth from the Father, who with the Father and the Son together is worshiped and glorified, who spake by the prophets. In one holy catholic and apostolic Church; we acknowledge one baptism for the remission of sins; we look for the resurrection of the dead, and the life of the world to come. Amen."*

The Council of Nicaea in 325 A.D. addressed the doctrine of Arianism head on. However, it all but ignored the Oneness/Monarchianism doctrine of Sabellius. As a matter of fact, there were a number of similarities to Sabellianism in this first Creed. The Constantinople Creed of 381 A.D. however, totally abandoned any and all association with the Monarchian doctrine of Sabellius.

Two other creeds were developed in the mid to late fifth century. The Athanasian Creed read, *"Whosoever will be saved, before all things it is necessary that he hold the catholic faith. Which faith unless every one do keep whole and undefiled, without doubt he shall perish everlastingly. And the catholic faith is this: that we worship one God in Trinity, and Trinity in Unity; neither confounding the Persons, nor dividing the Essence. For there is one Person of the Father; another of the Son; and another of the Holy Ghost. But the Godhead of the Father, of the Son, and of the Holy Ghost, is all one; the Glory equal, the Majesty coeternal. Such as the Father is; such is the Son; and such is the Holy Ghost. The Father uncreated; the Son uncreated; and the Holy Ghost uncreated. The Father unlimited; the Son unlimited; and the Holy Ghost unlimited. The Father eternal; the Son eternal; and the Holy Ghost eternal. And yet they are not three eternals; but one eternal. As also there are not three uncreated; nor three infinites, but one uncreated; and one infinite. So likewise the Father is Almighty; the Son Almighty; and the Holy Ghost Almighty. And yet they are not three Almighties; but one Almighty. So the Father is God; the Son is God; and the Holy Ghost is God. And yet they are not three Gods; but one God. So likewise the Father is Lord; the Son Lord; and the Holy Ghost Lord. And yet not three Lords; but one Lord. For like as we are compelled by the*

Christian verity; to acknowledge every Person by himself to be God and Lord; So are we forbidden by the catholic religion; to say, There are three Gods, or three Lords. The Father is made of none; neither created, nor begotten. The Son is of the Father alone; not made, nor created; but begotten. The Holy Ghost is of the Father and of the Son; neither made, nor created, nor begotten; but proceeding. So there is one Father, not three Fathers; one Son, not three Sons; one Holy Ghost, not three Holy Ghosts. And in this Trinity none is before, or after another; none is greater, or less than another. But the whole three Persons are coeternal, and coequal. So that in all things, as aforesaid; the Unity in Trinity, and the Trinity in Unity, is to be worshipped. He therefore that will be saved, let him thus think of the Trinity. Furthermore, it is necessary to everlasting salvation; that he also believe faithfully the Incarnation of our Lord Jesus Christ. For the right Faith is, that we believe and confess; that our Lord Jesus Christ, the Son of God, is God and Man; God, of the Substance [Essence] of the Father; begotten before the worlds; and Man, of the Substance [Essence] of his Mother, born in the world. Perfect God; and perfect Man, of a reasonable soul and human flesh subsisting. Equal to the Father, as touching his Godhead; and inferior to the Father as touching his Manhood. Who although he is God and Man; yet he is not two, but one Christ. One; not by conversion of the Godhead into flesh; but by assumption of the Manhood into God. One altogether; not by confusion of Substance [Essence]; but by unity of Person. For as the reasonable soul and flesh is one man; so God and Man is one Christ; Who suffered for our salvation; descended into hell; rose again the third day from the dead. He ascended into heaven, he sitteth on the right hand of God the Father Almighty, from whence he will come to judge the living and the dead. At whose coming all men will rise again with their bodies; And shall give account for their own works. And they that have done good shall go into life everlasting; and they that have done evil, into everlasting fire. This is the catholic faith; which except a man believe truly and firmly, he cannot be saved."

The Apostle's Creed read, *"I believe in God, the Father Almighty, Creator of Heaven and earth; and in Jesus Christ, His only Son Our Lord, Who was conceived by the Holy Spirit, born of the Virgin Mary, suffered under Pontius Pilate, was crucified, died, and was buried. He descended into Hell; the third day He rose again from the dead; He ascended into Heaven, and sitteth at the right hand of God, the Father almighty; from thence He shall come to judge the living and the dead. I believe in the Holy Spirit, the holy Catholic Church, the communion of saints, the forgiveness of sins, the resurrection of the body and life everlasting."*

Man-made traditions. In addition to accepting the Trinity Doctrine, the Catholic Church began practicing a series of man-made traditions. One of those traditions was the selling Indulgences, which was a way of reducing the amount of punishment one has to undergo for sins. Another tradition was the adoration of icons, statues and painted portraits, such that it came dangerously close to idolatry, which was a violation of the first commandment. From about the 3rd century and onward, infant baptism became standard practice in the Church. Papal primacy developed into a doctrine that the pope, as Bishop of Rome, has the divined authority delegated from Jesus to rule over the entire Christian Church. Papal Infallibility was a dogma stating that in virtue of the promise Jesus made to Peter, the pope is preserved from the possibility of error on doctrine and beliefs handed down to the Church. Salvation evolved to the point of requiring good works, baptism, participation in sacraments, penance, indulgences, and keeping the commandments. And then, there was the Immaculate Conception of Mary, the mother of Jesus. This church doctrine held that Mary was free of the original sin from the moment of conception.

Protestant Reformation splits the Church. The Protestant Reformation of the 16th century came about as a protest of many of the Catholic Church's man-made traditions. Martin Luther, John Calvin, Ulrich Zwingli, Jacobus Arminius, and Michael Servetus were some of the primary reformers. The Bible was translated into languages that provided access to Scripture by the common everyday Christian. The reformers taught that Salvation and eternal life are not earned by good deeds, but are received only as the free gift of God's grace through the believer's faith in Jesus Christ the redeemer, from sin. This Protestant Reformation resulted in the myriad of Christian denominations we see today.

Can non-Catholics be saved? The Second Vatican Council was held during four sessions of 8 to 12 weeks between 1962 and 1965. A portion of the Lumen Gentium 16 (LG 16) reads,

"Those who, through no fault of their own, do not know the Gospel of Christ, or his Church, but who nevertheless seek God with a sincere heart, and moved by grace, try in their actions to do his will as they know it through the dictates of their conscience—those, too, may achieve eternal salvation. Nor shall Divine Providence deny the assistance necessary for salvation to those who, without any fault of theirs, have not yet arrived at an explicit knowledge of God, and who, not without his grace, strive to live a good life. Whatever good or truth is found amongst them is considered by the Church to be a preparation for the Gospel, and given by him who enlightens all men so that they may finally have life."*

While this appears to indicate that Catholics believe non-Catholics can be saved, LG 14 is not quite so open to that possibility. It reads, *"This Sacred Council wishes to turn its attention firstly to the Catholic faithful. Basing itself upon Sacred Scripture and Tradition, it teaches that the Church, now sojourning on earth as an exile, is necessary for salvation. Christ, present to us in His Body, which is the Church, is the one Mediator and the unique way of salvation. In explicit terms He Himself affirmed the necessity of faith and baptism and thereby affirmed also the necessity of the Church, for through baptism as through a door men enter the Church.* ***Whosoever, therefore, knowing that the Catholic Church was made necessary by Christ, would refuse to enter or to remain in it, could not be saved.***"

---

[1] Letter to the Smyraeans, Chapter 8, Verse 2

[2] See "The Story of the Jews: Volume 12" by Larry J Tate for more information on Ignatius and his letters to the Church.

[3] Early Church Texts Nicene Creed 325

[4] Edict by Emperor Constantine against the Arians.

[5] The Council of Jerusalem in 335 A.D., Source: Athanasius De Synodis, Part 2, Section 21.

[6] Second Sirmium Confession

[7] Council of Constantinople in 360 A.D., Source: Athanasius De Synodis, Part 2, Section 30.

[8] Edict of Thessalonica

Lutheran

Martin Luther's Protestant Reformation begins. Martin Luther 1483-1546 A.D., was a German professor of theology, and is best known as a ground-breaking figure in the Protestant Reformation. He is also the namesake of the Lutheran Church. Luther was ordained to the priesthood in 1507, but before long, he came to reject several teachings and practices of the Roman Catholic Church. In particular, he disputed the Catholic view on Salvation and Indulgences.

Salvation. Luther taught that Salvation and eternal life are not earned by good deeds, but are received only as the free gift of God's grace through the believer's faith in Jesus Christ, the redeemer from sin. Luther insisted on the terms, "Christian," or "Evangelical," as the only acceptable names for individuals who professed Christ.

Luther came to view the use of terms such as "penance," and "righteousness," by the Catholic Church in new ways. He became convinced that the Church was corrupt in its ways, and had lost sight of what he saw as several of the central truths of Christianity. The most important for Luther was the doctrine of justification—God's act of declaring a sinner righteous by faith alone, through God's grace. He began to teach that Salvation, or redemption, is a gift of God's grace, attainable only through faith in Jesus as the Messiah. "*This one and firm rock, which we call the doctrine of justification*", he writes, "*is the chief article of the whole Christian doctrine, which comprehends the understanding of all godliness.*"

Luther came to understand justification as entirely the work of God. This teaching by Luther was clearly expressed in his 1525 A.D. publication, "On the Bondage of the Will." Luther wrote that Christians receive such righteousness entirely from outside themselves, and that righteousness not only comes from Christ, but actually *is* the righteousness of Christ, imputed to Christians through faith. "*That is why faith alone makes someone just and fulfills the law,*" he wrote. "*Faith is that which brings the Holy Spirit through the merits of Christ.*" Faith, for Luther, was a gift from God. The experience of being justified by faith was "*as though I had been born again.*" His entry into Paradise, no less, was a discovery about "the righteousness of God"—a discovery that "the just person" of whom the Bible speaks, lives by faith.[1] He explains his concept of "justification" in the Smalcald Articles: *"The first and chief article is this: Jesus Christ, our God and Lord, died for our sins and was raised again for our justification.[2] He alone is the Lamb of God who takes away the sins of the world,[3] and God has laid on Him the iniquity of us all.[4] All have sinned and are justified freely, without their own works and merits, by His grace, through the redemption that is in Christ Jesus, in His blood.[5] This is necessary to believe. This cannot be otherwise acquired or grasped by any work, law or merit. Therefore, it is clear and certain that this faith alone justifies us ... Nothing of this article can be yielded or surrendered, even though heaven and earth and everything else falls."*[6]

Luther's theology of justification was based on the process by which one is made right, or righteous, in the eyes of God. In Catholic theology, one is made righteous by a progressive infusion of grace accepted through faith, and cooperated with, through good works. Luther's doctrine of justification differed from Catholic theology in that justification meant "the declaring of one to be righteous," where God imputes the merits of Christ upon one who remains without inherent merit. In this process, good works are more of an unessential byproduct that contribute nothing to one's own state of righteousness.

Luther's rediscovery of Christ and his Salvation, was the first of two points that became the foundation for the Protestant Reformation.

Indulgences and the Ninety-five Theses. In 1516 A.D., Johann Tetzel, a Dominican friar, was sent to Germany by the Roman Catholic Church to sell indulgences to raise money for the rebuilding St. Peter's Basilica in Rome. Tetzel was known to say, "*As soon as a coin in the coffer rings, the soul from purgatory springs.*" On October 31, 1517, Luther wrote to his bishop, Albrecht von Brandenburg, protesting the sale of indulgences. He insisted that since forgiveness was God's alone to grant, those who claimed that indulgences absolved buyers from all punishments, and granted them Salvation, were in error. He included in his letter, a copy of his "Disputation on the Power and Efficacy of Indulgences," which became known as the "Ninety-five Theses." Thesis 86 asked, "*Why does the Pope, whose wealth today is greater than the wealth of the richest Crassus, build the basilica of St. Peter with the money of poor believers rather than with his own money?*" Next,

Luther posted another copy of the Ninety-five Theses on the door of All Saints' Church in Wittenberg. Then, in January, 1518, Luther had many copies of the Ninety-five Theses printed and distributed throughout Germany for all the people to read.

Luther is excommunicated. Pope Leo X instructed Dominican theologian Sylvester Mazzolini to draft a heresy case against Luther, and then summon Luther to a session of questioning. Over a three-day period in October 1518, Luther defended himself under questioning by papal legate Cardinal Cajetan. The Pope's right to issue indulgences was at the center of the dispute between the two men, and the hearings degenerated into a shouting match. "*His Holiness abuses Scripture,*" retorted Luther. "*I deny that he is above Scripture.*" Cajetan's original instructions had been to arrest Luther if he failed to recant, but he abstained from doing so. With help from the Carmelite monk Chrisoph Langenmantel, Luther slipped out of the city at night, unbeknownst to Cajetan. Luther's boldest assertion in the debate was that Matthew 16:18 does not confer on the Pope, the exclusive right to interpret scripture, and therefore, neither Popes, nor church councils were infallible.

After a number of debate sessions with representatives of the Pope, it was decided that Luther would not budge from his position. On June 15, 1520, the Pope warned Luther with the papal bull, "Exsurge Domine," that he risked excommunication within the next 60 days, unless he recanted forty-one sentences drawn from his writings, including the Ninety-five Theses. But, in open defiance to the Pope, Luther publicly set fire to the bull at Wittenberg on December 10, 1520. As a consequence, in the bull, "Decet Romanum Pontificem," Luther was excommunicated by Pope Leo X on January 3, 1521. The enforcement of the ban on the Ninety-five Theses fell to secular authorities.

On 18 April 1521, Luther appeared as ordered before the Diet of Worms. This was a general assembly of the estates of the Holy Roman Empire that took place in Worms, a town on the Rhine River. It was conducted from January 28th to May 25th, 1521, with Emperor Charles V presiding. Johann Eck, speaking on behalf of the empire, presented Luther with copies of his writings laid out on a table, and asked him if the books were his, and whether he stood by their contents. Luther confirmed he was their author but requested time to think about the answer to the second question. He prayed, consulted friends, and gave his response the next day, saying *"Unless I am convinced by the testimony of the Scriptures, or by clear reason, for I do not trust either in the pope or in councils alone, since it is well known that they have often erred and contradicted themselves, I am bound by the Scriptures I have quoted and my conscience is captive to the Word of God. I cannot, and will not recant anything, since it is neither safe nor right to go against conscience. May God help me. Amen."*

After Luther seemed to mock the proceedings, Eck informed him that he was acting like a heretic, and said, *"Martin, there is no one of the heresies which have torn the bosom of the church, which has not derived its origin from the various interpretation of the Scripture. The Bible itself is the arsenal whence each innovator has drawn his deceptive arguments. It was with Biblical texts that Pelagius and Arius maintained their doctrines..."*

Over the next five days, private conferences were held to determine Luther's fate. The emperor presented the final draft of the Edict of Worms on May 25, 1521, excommunicating Luther, declaring him an outlaw, banning his literature, and requiring his arrest. The edict read, *"For this reason we forbid anyone from this time forward to dare, either by words or by deeds, to receive, defend, sustain, or favour the said Martin Luther. On the contrary, we want him to be apprehended and punished as a notorious heretic, as he deserves, to be brought personally before us, or to be securely guarded until those who have captured him inform us, whereupon we will order the appropriate manner of proceeding against the said Luther. Those who will help in his capture will be rewarded generously for their good work."*

The papal bull also made it a crime for anyone in Germany to give Luther food or shelter, and it permitted anyone to kill Luther without legal consequence. To Martin's good fortune, some of his sympathizers spirited him away to the security of the Wartburg Castle at Eisenach, which Martin referred to as, *"My Patmos."*

Translation of the Bible into German. While at the Wartburg Castle, Martin busied himself with translating the New Testament from Greek to German, and wrote a number of doctrinal writings. By 1526, Luther found himself increasingly occupied in organizing a new church, in addition to translating the Bible. He finished translating the New Testament in 1522, and the Old Testament in 1534. His translation of the Bible from

Latin to German made it more accessible to the common Christian, an event that had a tremendous impact on both the Church and German culture.

The Lutheran Church comes into being. The Lutheran Church became an official organization around 1530 A.D. Then, in 1546, Luther died with Pope Leo X's excommunication still in effect, and the Catholic Church has never lifted that 1520 excommunication.

Lutheran beliefs. Traditionally, Lutherans hold the Bible to be divinely inspired, and the only Spiritual basis for Christian teaching. Lutherans believe there are no deficiencies in Scripture that need to be supplemented by tradition, new revelations, or evolving doctrine. The Lutheran Church sees itself as the church founded by Christ and the Apostles, and that during the Reformation, the Catholic Church fell away.

As for Salvation, Lutherans believe people are saved from their sins by Faith and Grace alone. Lutherans believe baptism to be a saving work of God, mandated and instituted by Jesus Christ. To Lutherans, baptism is a means of grace through which God creates and strengthens saving faith. Like Catholics, Lutherans believe in infant baptism. Lutherans hold fast to the Scripture, "*The like figure whereunto even baptism doth also now save us (not the putting away of the filth of the flesh, but the answer of a good conscience toward God,) by the resurrection of Jesus Christ.*"[7]

As for the Godhead, Lutherans are strictly Trinitarian, and adhere to the Nicene Creed, the Apostles' Creed, and the Athanasian Creed.

The typical Lutheran church service is somewhat rigid, generally consisting of the congregation corporately reciting Scriptures, a sermon, a recitation of either the Apostles' Creed or the Nicene Creed, prayers, and communion. Some Lutheran churches now hold contemporary worship services, a form of worship originally confined to the charismatic movement.

---

[1] Rom. 1:17

[2] Rom. 3:24-25

[3] John 1:29

[4] Isa. 53:6

5 Rom. 3:23-25

6 Mark 13:31

7 1 Pet. 3:21

Mennonite

Overview. The Mennonites descended from the Anabaptist denominations, and were named after Menno Simons. Today's Mennonites are split according to their beliefs. Some describe themselves as a religious denomination, while others hold on to being both an ethnic group and a religious denomination. Congregations worldwide vary from being "plain people," to those who are indistinguishable in dress and appearance from the general population.

History. The early history of the Mennonites begins with the Anabaptists in German and Dutch-speaking portions of Europe. The most distinguishing feature of the Anabaptists, was their rejection of infant baptism being performed in the Catholic Church. In the early 1500's Menno Simmons, a Catholic priest, heard of the Anabaptist movement, and started to rethink his Catholic faith. In 1536, he left the Roman Catholic Church, and became a leader in the Anabaptist movement. By 1540, he rose to a high rank in the Anabaptist society, and by 1544, he had his own following of people who called themselves, "Mennonites." A strong sense of "community" became typical of Mennonite churches, and they learned to live very simply.

In 1693, Jakob Ammann led an effort to reform the Mennonite Church. When his efforts failed, Ammann and his followers split from the Mennonites, and became known as, "Amish Mennonites," or just "Amish."

Worship and traditions. Today, there is a wide variation of worship, doctrine, and traditions among the Mennonites due to many splits, and the formation of other Mennonite groups.

Moderate Mennonites, such as the Mennonite Brethren, differ very little from other Protestant congregations. There is no special form of dress, and no restrictions on technology. Worship services typically consist of singing, scripture reading, prayer, and a sermon. The distinguishing characteristics of moderate Mennonite churches tend to be an emphasis on peace, community, and service. However, members do not live in a separate community. Service in the military is generally not permitted.

Conservative Mennonites see themselves as true followers of Menno Simon's teachings, and they insist on dressing in conservative clothing. They do not believe the use of modern technology is a sin, but they discourage extensive use of the Internet, and avoid the use of television, cameras, and radio.

Old Order Mennonites are split into a number of groups. Some groups use horse and buggy for transportation, and speak German, while others drive cars and speak English. What most Old Orders share in common, is conservative doctrine, dress, and traditions. They refuse to participate in politics and other so-called sins of the world. Most of the Old Order Mennonites school their children in Mennonite-operated schools.

There are some progressive Mennonite churches that allow LGBTQ members to worship as church members. They go so far as to ordain LGBTQ leaders.

There are hundreds or thousands of Mennonite churches and groups, many of which are separate from all others. Some churches are members of regional or area conferences, and some of these conferences are affiliated with larger national or international conferences. There is no single world authority among the Mennonites.

Presbyterian

History. Presbyterianism is a part of the Reformed tradition of John Calvin within Protestantism that traces its roots to the Church of Scotland. Presbyterian theology typically emphasizes the sovereignty of God, the authority of the Scriptures, and the necessity of Grace through faith in Christ. The roots of Presbyterianism are tied to the Protestant Reformation of the 16th century, specifically, 1560 when the First Book of Discipline was published.

Doctrine. Presbyterianism is historically a confessional tradition in which the members express their faith in the form of, "Confessions of faith." The Presbyterian Church of the USA has adopted the, "Book of Confessions," which reflects the inclusion of other Reformed confessions, in addition to the Westminster Standards. These documents include the Nicene Creed, the Apostles' Creed, and other confessions.

Worship. The worship services of the Presbyterians include the singing of hymns, preaching, and congregational participation

Unitarianism

Unitarianism developed in Poland as a result of a controversy in 1556 that started when Peter Gonesius spoke out against the doctrine of the Trinity during a meeting of Calvinist churches. In 1565, after nine years of debate, the anti-Trinitarians were excluded from their church, and began forming their own church organization.

Unitarianism is a non-trinitarian Christian movement which believes God is one singular entity, as opposed to the Trinity doctrine which does not adhere to strict monotheism. Unitarians maintain that Jesus was inspired by God, a great man, and a prophet of God, perhaps even a savior, but he was not a deity, or God incarnate. The Unitarian movement has never accepted the Godhood of Jesus, and therefore does not agree with the non-trinitarian belief systems that do, such as Oneness Pentecostalism and the United Pentecostal Church International.

Unitarians believe the authors of the Bible were inspired by God, but as humans, they were subject to human error.

Unitarianism is also known for its rejection of several mainstream doctrines, including the doctrine of the original sin and the infallibility of the Bible. Therefore, Unitarianism can be placed among churches known for liberalism.

By way of reason, science, philosophy, Scripture, and other religions, Unitarians have developed liberal views of God, Jesus, the world, and the purpose of life. They believe reason and Christian belief are complimentary. Human nature is neither inherently corrupt, nor depraved, but capable of both good and evil, just as God intended. Consequently, humans have the ability to exercise free will in a responsible, constructive, and ethical manner.

Episcopal

Overview. The Episcopal Church is a Protestant Denomination, and a member of the worldwide Anglican Communion. The church was organized after the American Revolution when it became separate from the Church of England. The Church describes itself as Protestant, yet Catholic, and claims apostolic succession, tracing its bishops back to the Apostles. However, the Catholic Church does not recognize that claim. About three-quarters of the signers of the Declaration of Independence were affiliated with the Episcopal Church, and over a quarter of all Presidents of the United States have been Episcopalians. Since the 1960's and 1970's, the church has drifted along a more liberal course, calling for equality of homosexuals, and going so far as to approve of same-sex marriages.

History. The Episcopal Church has its origins in the Church of England in the American colonies. The first parish was founded in Jamestown, Virginia in 1607, but at that time, it was still under the umbrella of the Church of England. The Revolutionary War divided both the clergy and laity of the Church of England in America, especially due to the fact that three-quarters of the signers of the Declaration of Independence were Anglican laymen. In 1789, the Episcopal Church formally separated from the Church of England.

In 1976, the Episcopal Church affirmed that homosexuals have the right to participate in the church, and the first homosexual person was ordained as a priest in 1977, and the first homosexual bishop was elected in 2003.

Beliefs. Episcopalians believe in the teachings and resurrection of Jesus Christ, along with the Apostles' and Nicene Creeds, and the Trinity of the Godhead. They believe that Grace is God's favor toward man, and it is unearned and undeserved.

Baptist

Origins of the Baptist Church. There are a number of conflicting views regarding the origin of the Baptist Church. One is that the Baptist Church began in the year 1609 in Amsterdam with pastor John Smyth, who made the decision to reject the wide-spread practice of the baptizing infants, and instead, instituted baptism only to adults who confessed their belief in Jesus Christ. Another claim is that the Baptist Church was an outgrowth of the Anabaptist movement which began in 1525. Finally, some believe the Baptist faith has continually existed since the time of Christ.

The first Baptists churches established in the United States were in 1639 when Roger Williams founded a Baptist church in Providence, Rhode Island, and John Clarke began a Baptist church in Newport, Rhode Island.

In 1845, the United Baptist congregations split over controversies associated with slavery and missions. This split resulted in the creation of the Southern Baptist Convention, which supported slavery, and the American Baptists Churches USA, who opposed slavery.

Beliefs and Ordinances of the Baptist Church. Baptists generally observe two ordinances: the Lord's Supper, and Believer's Baptism. Christian believers only, are allowed to be baptized, and then, only by complete immersion.

Baptists believe in one God, the virgin birth, miracles, the Trinity of the Godhead, the need for Salvation through faith in Jesus Christ, and the Second Coming of Jesus Christ. Other beliefs tend to vary among Baptists, such as the Second Work of Grace, speaking in tongues, and which translation of the Bible that should be used.

Some Baptists lean toward Calvinist teachings which hold that God predestined some people to be saved, while others are predestined to eternal damnation. Other Baptists are Arminian, believing that salvation is available to any believer who makes the choice to respond positively to God, and accept Jesus into their life.

Most Baptists believe in Eternal Security, also known as the "Perseverance of the Saints," or "Once Saved, Always Saved."

A few of the Scriptural passages Baptists use to support their belief in Eternal Security are:

"Verily, verily, I say unto you, He that heareth my word, and believeth on him that sent me, hath everlasting life, and shall not come into condemnation; but is passed from death unto life." (John 5:24)

"And I give unto them eternal life; and they shall never perish, neither shall any man pluck them out of my hand." (John 10:28)

"These things have I written unto you that believe on the name of the Son of God; that ye may know that ye have eternal life, and that ye may believe on the name of the Son of God." (1 John 5:13)

The Southern Baptist Convention. The SBC is the world's largest Baptist denomination, the largest Protestant organization, and the second-largest Christian denomination in the United States, the first of which is the Roman Catholic Church.

The Southern Baptist Church formed as the result of their support of slavery in 1845. In order to rectify this situation of racial inequality, the Southern Baptist Convention passed a resolution in 1995 that recognized the failure of their predecessors to protect the civil rights of African Americans, and sought forgiveness for their previous wrongs. The resolution read in part, *"Our relationship to African-Americans has been hindered from the beginning by the role that slavery played in the formation of the Southern Baptist Convention. Many of our Southern Baptist forbears defended the right to own slaves, and either participated in, supported, or acquiesced in the particularly inhumane nature of American slavery. In later years Southern Baptists failed, in many cases, to support, and in some cases opposed, legitimate initiatives to secure the civil rights of African-Americans. Racism has led to discrimination, oppression, injustice, and violence, both in the Civil War and throughout the history of our nation. Racism has divided the body of Christ and Southern Baptists in particular, and separated us from our African-American brothers and sisters; and many of our congregations have intentionally and/or unintentionally excluded African-Americans from worship, membership, and leadership. Racism profoundly distorts our understanding of Christian morality, leading some Southern Baptists to believe that racial prejudice and discrimination are compatible with the Gospel. Jesus performed the ministry of reconciliation to restore sinners to a right relationship with the Heavenly Father, and to establish right relations among all human beings, especially within the family of faith."*

"Therefore, be it resolved that we…unwaveringly denounce racism, in all its forms, as deplorable sin; and that we affirm the Bibles teaching that every human life is sacred, and is of equal and immeasurable worth, made in Gods image, regardless of race or ethnicity (Genesis 1:27), and that, with respect to salvation through Christ, there is neither Jew nor Greek, there is neither slave nor free, there is neither male nor female, for (we) are all one in Christ Jesus (Galatians 3:28). We lament and repudiate historic acts of evil such as slavery from which we continue to reap a bitter harvest, and we recognize that the racism which yet plagues our culture today is inextricably tied to the past; and we apologize to all African-Americans for condoning and/or perpetuating individual and systemic racism in our lifetime; and we genuinely repent of racism of which we have been guilty, whether consciously (Psalm 19:13) or unconsciously (Leviticus 4:27); and we ask forgiveness from our African-American brothers and sisters,

acknowledging that our own healing is at stake. We hereby commit ourselves to eradicate racism in all its forms from Southern Baptist life and ministry; and we commit ourselves to be doers of the Word (James 1:22) by pursuing racial reconciliation in all our relationships, especially with our brothers and sisters in Christ (1 John 2:6), to the end that our light would so shine before others, that they may see (our) good works and glorify (our) Father in heaven (Matthew 5:16). We pledge our commitment to the Great Commission task of making disciples of all people (Matthew 28:19), confessing that in the church God is calling together one people from every tribe and nation (Revelation 5:9), and proclaiming that the Gospel of our Lord Jesus Christ is the only certain and sufficient ground upon which redeemed persons will stand together in restored family union as joint-heirs with Christ (Romans 8:17)."

Speaking in Tongues. Historically, the Southern Baptist Convention has not considered speaking in tongues (Glossolalia) to be in accordance with Scriptural teaching. However, the Baptist Faith and Message (BF&M), does not specifically mention it. Baptists are not generally of one mind when it comes to the issue of speaking in tongues. Some Baptists consider themselves to be "Cessationists," who believe speaking in tongues fulfilled a specific purpose through the Apostles in the 1st century, and then ceased after their death. Others are "Continualists," who believe that all the miraculous gifts continue to be active today. Over all however, most Baptists congregations do not practice speaking in tongues during public worship, leaving that particular Spiritual gift to times of private prayer only.

Quaker

Origin. After becoming dissatisfied with the teachings of the Church of England George Fox claimed to have had a divine revelation that a person can have a direct experience with Christ without the aid of ordained clergy, which led to allegations of blasphemy. In 1650, Fox stood before Gervase Bennet of the House of Commons and suggested that Bennet should tremble at the Word of the Lord. Thus, the term "Quaker" was coined.

By 1656, a group of Quakers migrated to North America, and began preaching in Boston where they were accused of heresy because of their insistence on obedience to the "Inner Light," a belief that the Spirit of God was in them. Consequently, they were imprisoned for five weeks, then banished. Their books were burned, and their property confiscated. One Quaker was hanged for defying the banishment and remaining in the Boston area. After this, groups of Quakers made their way to New Jersey, Rhode Island, Pennsylvania, North Carolina, Maryland, and Virginia, and became known as the Society of Friends.

In the 18th century, some Quakers split from the main Society of Friends over issues such as Conscientious Objection to serving in war, and formed the Free Quakers, Universal Friends, and other groups. Later, in the 19th and 20th centuries more splits occurred over theological beliefs.

Theology. The theological beliefs of Quakers vary considerably. Most Friends believe in "Continuing Revelation," the belief that God continuously reveals truth directly to individuals. They reject the idea of priests, and instead, believe in the priesthood of all believers. Most Quakers don't believe baptism is necessary. They do believe in the Trinitarian concept of the Father, Son, and Holy Spirit, but the roles played by each Person of the Godhead varies widely among Quakers.

Various splintered groups. The group known as Conservative Friends are conservative in their beliefs, believing they are truest to the original Quaker doctrine. They use plain language, plain dress, and tend to live in villages and rural areas. Evangelical Friends have religious beliefs that are similar to other evangelical Christians, having a mission to evangelize the unsaved of the world, to transform them spiritually through God's love, and through social service to others. Unlike more conservative Quakers, the Evangelical Friends partake in sacraments, and teach baptism by immersion. The Gurneyites, also known as Friends United Meeting, account for about 49 percent of worldwide Quakers. They are followers of Evangelical Quaker theology that Jesus is their teacher and Lord, and they favor close work with other Protestant churches. Holiness Friends are influenced by the Holiness movement. Liberal Quakerism refers to Friends who share a mix of theological ideas such as a Social Gospel. They highlight the importance of good works, living simply, and telling the truth. Universalist Friends claim there are different pathways to God, and it doesn't matter if one is a Christian, Muslim, Hindu, or of some other belief. The Non-theist Friends are predominantly atheists, agnostics, and humanists who still value membership in a religious organization.

Other facts about Quakers. Quaker groups are scattered around the globe, but they are very few in number, estimated to be between 300,000 and 400,000 worldwide. Two U.S. presidents were Quakers: Herbert Hoover, and Richard Nixon.

Amish

Overview. The Amish are Christian believers who originated from among the Anabaptists, and are closely related to Mennonite churches. The Amish are known for simple living, plain dress and their slowness to adopt many of the conveniences of modern technology. Maintaining self-sufficiency is of utmost importance to the Amish.

History. The Amish church began with a schism in Switzerland within a group of Swiss and Alsatian Mennonite Anabaptists in 1693. In the second half of the 19th century, the Amish divided into Old Order Amish and Amish Mennonites, a more liberal group that adopted the use of motor cars. When people refer to the Amish today, they normally refer to the Old Order Amish. In the early 18th century, many Amish and Mennonites immigrated to Pennsylvania which was known for its lack of religious persecution, as well as attractive land offers.

Religious practices. Amish church membership begins with adult baptism. Church worship services are generally held every other Sunday in a member's home or barn. The rules of the church must be observed by every member, and covers many aspects of day-to-day living, including prohibitions or limitations on the use of power-line electricity, telephones, and automobiles, as well as regulations on clothing. The Amish typically operate their own schools and discontinue formal education after grade eight. Most Amish do not buy commercial insurance or participate in Social Security. Amish church members practice non-resistance and will not perform any type of military service.

Way of Life. Bearing children, raising them, and socializing with neighbors and relatives are the greatest functions of the Amish family. Amish typically believe that large families are a blessing from God. Farm families tend to have larger families, because sons are needed to perform farm labor. Community is central to the Amish way of life.

Working hard is considered godly, and some technological advancements have been considered undesirable because they reduce the need for hard work. Machines such as automatic floor cleaners in barns have historically been rejected as this provides young farmhands with too much free time.

The Amish are known for their plain attire. Men wear solid colored shirts, broad-brimmed hats, and suits that signify similarity amongst one another. Amish men grow beards to symbolize manhood and marital status, as well as to promote humility. They are forbidden to grow mustaches because mustaches are seen by the Amish as being affiliated with the military. Women have similar guidelines on how to dress. They are to wear calf-length dresses, muted colors along with bonnets and aprons. Prayer caps or bonnets are worn by the women because they are a visual representation of their religious beliefs and promote unity through the tradition of every woman wearing one. The color of the bonnet signifies whether a woman is single or married. Single women wear black bonnets and married women wear white. The color coding of bonnets is important because women are not allowed to wear jewelry, such as wedding rings, as it is seen as drawing attention to the body which can induce pride in the individual. All clothing is sewn by hand.

Methodist

The Methodist movement begins. John Wesley was an English clergyman, theologian, and evangelist who was a leader of a revival movement within the Church of England. He led the "Holy Club" in Oxford England where he had been educated. This club was formed for the purpose of the study and pursuit of a devout Christian life. Meeting daily from six to nine, the club members prayed, read psalms, and read from the Greek New Testament. In 1732, an anonymous pamphlet was published, describing Wesley and his group as "The Oxford Methodists."

Wesley believed the formal Church of England was failing to call sinners to repentance, and many of the clergy were corrupt, resulting in people perishing in their sins. Furthermore, he believed he had been commissioned by God to bring about revival in the Church. In 1738, Wesley experienced his own evangelical conversion, when in a time of prayer, he felt his heart strangely warmed. This is when the Methodism movement formally began.

Martin Luther may be known for kick-starting the Protestant Reformation, but John Wesley, the founder of the Methodist Church, is often viewed as the father of the modern Holiness and Pentecostal movements. Wesley is the one who developed the doctrine of sinless perfectionism, otherwise known as the "second blessing" of the believer. According to Wesley, this perfectionism was something a believer must seek and strive for.

Approximately 200 years before John Wesley's time, Martin Luther had determined that the Catholic Church had drifted away from the teachings of the original Apostolic Church. In a similar manner, Wesley believed that the Church of England had also drifted away from the original Church. A commandment in the Book of Mark was the primary motivation behind his new doctrine. *"And thou shalt love the Lord thy God with all thy heart, and with all thy soul, and with all thy mind, and with all thy strength: this is the first commandment. And the second is like, namely this, Thou shalt love thy neighbour as thyself. There is none other commandment greater than these."* (Mark 12:30-31)

John Wesley taught that Christians should live a life of Christian holiness, which means that a believer is to love God with all one's heart, soul, mind and strength, and to love one's neighbor as oneself. This new doctrine came to be known as Wesleyanism. John Wesley believed that to be made perfect in love meant that Christians should not only love God, but they should help others as well.

Wesley and his early Methodists were first and foremost, focused on inviting people to experience God's grace, which is often defined as the love and mercy given to us by God, because God wants us to have it, not because of anything we have done to earn it. Then, the new converts were instructed to grow in their knowledge and love of God by way of disciplined Christian living. Wesley's primary emphasis was on Christian living, and on putting their faith into action.

According to Wesley, Christian conversion is a turning around, the leaving of a life of sin, and pursuing a life with God. When a person does this, he experiences justification from God. Then, once he is justified, it is the Christian's responsibility not only to love God, but to actively love his neighbor as well. This is considered to be God's active presence in our lives.

Modern Methodist beliefs. Methodism teaches that Salvation begins when a convert chooses to respond to God, and believe in him. After the new birth, converts are taught to pursue holiness, good works, and to remain in the faith. Should a person lose their faith through sinning (backsliding), they must confess their sins and be sanctified again in order to return to God. Methodists declare the Old and New Testaments to be the only divinely inspired Scripture, and the primary source of authority for Christians.

The United Methodist Church encourages its members to be involved in outreach and evangelism, and to seek holiness by the power of the Holy Spirit. The Apostles' Creed, as well as the Nicene Creed are used frequently in worship services. The church believes the Trinitarian formula of baptism is a sign of Christian profession, as well as a sign of the new birth a convert has received.

The Methodist Church supports the abstinence from alcohol, but seems to stop short of an outright prohibition. As for the theory of evolution, there is a move within the organization to distance itself from biblical creationism, saying they find that science's descriptions of biological evolution are not in conflict with theology. Gambling is considered to be a sin, therefore opposed by the church. Heated debates over the acceptance of sexual orientation issues and homosexuality are now threatening to split the United Methodist Church into two denominations, with one group in favor of homosexuality, and the other entirely opposed to it.

Methodist Denominations. There are many Methodist denominations, each having their own unique beliefs and lifestyle standards. A merger in 1968 created the United Methodist Church, resulting in it being the largest Methodist denomination. The United Methodist Church is the second largest Protestant church, behind the Southern Baptist Convention.

Christian Church (Disciples of Christ)

History. The Christian Church (Disciples of Christ) is so named because it started as two distinct but similar movements, each without knowledge of the other, in the early 19th century. The first of these two groups, led by Barton W. Stone began at Cane Ridge, Kentucky. The group called themselves simply Christians. The second, began in western Pennsylvania and Virginia (now West Virginia), led by Thomas Campbell and his son, Alexander Campbell. Because the founders wanted to abandon all denominational labels, they called themselves Disciples of Christ.

In 1804, Barton Stone and other like-minded people announced their withdrawal from Presbyterianism, which had been established by John Calvin during the Protestant Reformation. This new group had the intention of being simply the body of Christ. It wasn't long however, before they adopted the name, "Christian" to identify themselves.

About this same time, Thomas Campbell began publishing writings regarding his convictions about the Church of Jesus

Christ, emphasizing Christian unity and the restoration of the New Testament Church. They named their first church, "The Brush Run Church." When their study of the New Testament led the reformers to begin to practice baptism by immersion, the nearby Redstone Baptist Association invited Brush Run Church to join with them for the purpose of fellowship. The reformers agreed provided that they would be "allowed to preach and to teach whatever they learned from the Scriptures."

In 1832, the Christian Church merged with the Disciples of Christ, and early in the 20th century, the name of the newly merged organization eventually became known as the International Convention of Christian Churches (Disciples of Christ).

Beliefs. While there are differences in the nature of worship exhibited by various Christian churches, baptism, and confession of Christ as Lord, seems to a commonly held belief. Consequently, they consider baptism and acceptance of Jesus Christ as Lord to be essential to Salvation. Beyond the essential commitment to follow Jesus, there is a tremendous freedom of belief and interpretation. As the basic teachings of Jesus are studied and applied to life, there is the freedom to interpret

Jesus' teaching in different ways. As would be expected from such an approach, there is a wide diversity among Disciples in what individuals and congregations believe.

Worship. Most congregations sing hymns, read from the Old and New Testaments, hear the word of God proclaimed through sermon or other medium and extend an invitation to become Christ's Disciples. Most Disciple congregations practice weekly celebrations of the Lord's Supper. Communion is understood as the symbolic presence of Jesus within the gathered community.

Baptism. Most Disciple congregations practice believer's baptism in the form of immersion, believing it to be the form used in the New Testament. The experiences of yielding to Christ in being buried with him in the waters of baptism and rising to a new life, have profound meaning for the church. While most congregations exclusively practice baptism by immersion, some Disciples also accept other forms of baptism including infant baptism.

Homosexuality. In 1977, the General Assembly of the denomination debated resolutions about homosexuality, and a resolution condemning the "homosexual lifestyle" was defeated. At the next General Assembly two years later, the Assembly approved a resolution that condemned the ordination of homosexuals. At the same time, however, various regions of the church were given more freedom in how to handle homosexuals. Since then, some regions have ordained homosexual ministers.

Mormons

Overview. Mormonism was started by Joseph Smith during the 1820's. After Smith's death in 1844, the movement split into several groups. The majority followed Brigham Young, while other groups combined to become the Community of Christ.

The term, "Mormon" was originally coined to describe any person who believes in the Book of Mormon as a volume of Scripture. The largest sect of Mormons, based in Salt Lake City, prefers the term, "Latter Day Saints," also known as, "The Church of Jesus Christ of Latter-Day Saints (LDS Church).

History of the movement. Joseph Smith claimed that in 1823, he was directed by an angel to a hill near his home in Manchester, New York, where he found a buried stone box containing a set of golden plates, or thin metallic pages, which were engraved with hieroglyphics, and bound with three D-shaped rings. He said that the angel prevented him from taking the plates, but instructed him to return to the same location in a year. Smith returned to that site every year to look at the plates, but it wasn't until 1827 that he was permitted to take them home. Even then, he wasn't allowed to show the plates to anyone until he finished translating them to English. Then, after showing the plates to a few people, he returned the plates to the angel Moroni, and the plates were never seen again.

In 1830, Smith published the Book of Mormon, originally written by the prophet Mormon. This book consisted of the religious history of an ancient American civilization. With his Book of Mormon published, Smith founded what he called, "The Church of Christ," which later on, became known as the "Latter Day Saints."

By 1831, Smith's church began expanding westward, and he sought to build what he called, "The City of Zion," or "The New Jerusalem," in Missouri. However, Missouri's settlers became alarmed at this rapid influx of Mormons, and attempted to force them out. In 1838, tensions escalated into the Mormon War, and the Missouri governor declared the Mormons to be enemies and should be driven from the state. This edict resulted in thousands of Mormons migrating to Illinois.

In 1839, the Mormons converted some swampland on the banks of the Mississippi River, named the area Nauvoo,

Illinois, and began construction of the Nauvoo Temple. The city became the church's new headquarters and gathering place. Meanwhile, Smith published the story of his First Vision, in which the Father and the Son appeared to him when he was 14 years old. This vision eventually came to be regarded by some Mormons as the most important event in human history— after the birth, ministry, and resurrection of Jesus Christ.

In 1844, conflicts arose between Mormons and non-Mormons in both Illinois and Missouri. Smith was arrested, and on June 27, 1844, he and his brother Hyrum were killed by a mob in Carthage, Illinois. Brigham Young, a close associate of Smith, assumed leadership over the majority of the Latter Day Saints.

For two years after Joseph Smith's death, conflicts continued to escalate between Mormons and other Illinois residents. In order to prevent war, Brigham Young led the Mormon pioneers to temporary winter quarters in Nebraska, and then in 1847, they continued traveling to what would one day be called the Utah Territory. Having failed to build Zion within the borders of established American territories, the Mormons began constructing a society based on their beliefs and values in the isolation of Utah.

Mormon settlers soon branched out and colonized a region now known as the Mormon corridor, with each village governed by local Mormon bishops. The land was viewed as commonly owned, thus there was a co-operative system of irrigation that allowed them to build a prosperous farming community in the desert.

From 1849 to 1852, the Mormons expanded their missionary efforts, establishing several missions in Europe, Latin America, and the South Pacific. Converts were expected to gather to Zion, and thousands of Mormon converts immigrated to America, crossing the Great Plains in wagons drawn by oxen. Then, during the 1860's, newcomers began arriving via a newly-built railroad.

In 1852, church leaders publicized their previously-secret practice of polygamy. Over the next 50 years, many Mormons entered into plural marriages as a religious duty, with the number of plural marriages reaching a peak around 1860. The practice of polygamy made some degree of economic sense to the Mormons, because many of the plural wives were single women who arrived in Utah without brothers or fathers to offer them societal support.

By 1857, tensions had again escalated between Mormons and other Americans, largely as a result of accusations involving polygamy and their "divinely guided" rule of the Utah Territory by Brigham Young. President James Buchanan sent an army to Utah, which Mormons interpreted as open aggression against them. Fearing a repeat of the previous conflicts in Missouri and Illinois, the Mormons prepared to defend themselves, going so far as preparing to torch their own homes if they were invaded by the army. Fortunately, little conflict materialized, and in 1858, Young agreed to step down from his position as governor of the territory, and was replaced by a non-Mormon. Nevertheless, the LDS Church still wielded significant political power in the Utah Territory.

After Brigham Young's death in 1877, he was followed by other LDS Church presidents who resisted efforts by the United States Congress to outlaw Mormon polygamous marriages. In 1878, the U.S. Supreme Court ruled that religious duty was not a suitable defense for practicing polygamy, and many Mormon polygamists went into hiding, resulting in Congress issuing an order to begin seizing church assets. In September 1890, church president Wilford Woodruff issued a Manifesto that officially suspended the practice of polygamy. Although this Manifesto did not dissolve existing plural marriages, relations with the United States markedly improved after 1890. In spite of the Manifesto, some Mormons continued entering into polygamous marriages, but these eventually stopped in 1904 when church president Joseph F. Smith disavowed polygamy before Congress and issued a "Second Manifesto" calling for all plural marriages in the church to cease. Eventually, the church adopted a policy of excommunicating members found practicing polygamy.

The 20th century saw an effort by the Mormons to integrate into the American mainstream. In 1929, the Mormon Tabernacle Choir began broadcasting a weekly performance on national radio, and became an important asset for public relations. The Mormons emphasized patriotism and industry, and in so doing, they rose in status from the bottom of religious denominations to middle-class. The LDS Church grew rapidly after World War II and became a worldwide organization, as missionaries were sent across the globe. By 2012, there were an estimated 14.8 million Mormons.

Beliefs. Mormon converts are urged to undergo lifestyle changes, repent of sins, and adopt standards of conduct such as studying scriptures, praying daily, fasting regularly, attending Sunday worship services, participating in church programs and activities on weekdays, and refraining from work on Sundays when possible.

The most important part of the Mormon church service is considered to be the Lord's Supper, in which church members renew covenants made at baptism. Mormons also emphasize standards they believe were taught by Jesus Christ, including personal honesty, integrity, obedience to law, chastity outside marriage, and fidelity within marriage. Same-sex marriages are not performed or supported by the LDS Church.

Mormons have a scriptural canon consisting of the Bible (both Old and New Testaments), the Book of Mormon, and a collection of revelations and writings by Joseph Smith known as the Doctrine and Covenants and Pearl of Great Price. Mormons have a relatively open definition of Scripture, in that anything spoken or written by one of their prophets while under inspiration, is considered to be the Word of God.

Mormons believe God's aim is to bring his children to immortality and eternal life. God's most important plan involved Jesus, the eldest of God's children, coming to earth as the literal Son of God, to conquer sin and death so that God's other children could return. According to Mormons, every person who lives on earth will be resurrected, and nearly all of them will be received into various kingdoms of glory. To be accepted into the highest kingdom, however a person must fully accept Christ through faith, repentance, and through ordinances such as baptism and the laying on of hands.

A prominent practice among young and retired members of the LDS Church is to serve a proselytizing mission with a goal of building the church. Oftentimes, young, conservatively dressed Mormons will be seen riding bicycles through neighborhoods as they witness to others.

Godhead. Mormons believe the Father, Son, and Holy Ghost are three distinct beings, and the Father and Jesus have glorified, physical bodies—while the Holy Ghost is a spirit without a physical body. They also believe there are other gods and goddesses outside the Godhead, such as a Heavenly Mother—who is the wife of God the Father—and that faithful Latter-day Saints may attain their own godhood in the afterlife.

Seventh Day Adventists

Origins. The Seventh Day Adventist Church is a Protestant Christian denomination which is known for its observance of Saturday, the seventh day of the week, as the Sabbath, along with its emphasis on the imminent Second Coming of Jesus Christ. The Seventh Day Adventists Church is the largest of several Adventists groups which grew out of the Millerite Movement in the United States in the 1840's, and was formally established in 1863.

William Miller was a Baptist preacher who, after intensive studies of the prophecies of Daniel, especially Dan. 8:14, which reads, *"And he said unto me, Unto two thousand and three hundred days; then shall the sanctuary be cleansed,"* became convinced the Second Coming of Jesus Christ would occur sometime between March 21, 1843 and March 21, 1844. When these dates passed without incident, a new date was set, October 22, 1844. A great disappointment settled on the Millerites when Jesus did not return as expected in 1844. Some members rejoined their previous denominations, and others went on to form new denominations, one of which was the Seventh Day Adventists.

Beliefs. Along with many other Christian organizations, the Adventists teach the Trinity, the infallibility of Scripture, and baptism by immersion. A unique belief of the Adventists has to do with the Sabbath. On Saturdays, Adventists abstain from secular work, competitive sports, and watching non-religious programs on television. The major weekly worship service occurs on Saturday. Four times a year, after a foot washing ceremony, the Adventists partake in communion.

Some other Adventist beliefs include the Creation occurring in six literal days, the Annihilationist View of Hell, Investigative Judgment, and Legalism. Annihilationism is the belief that the wicked will perish or cease to exist. After the Last Judgment, all unsaved people will be totally destroyed so as to not exist, rather than suffering everlasting torment in hell.

The belief in Investigative Judgment came about after the Second Coming of Jesus failed to occur in 1844. After additional studies in the Book of Daniel, it was decided that 1844 A.D. had to do with Jesus moving from his first phase of ministry, called the Holy Place, to the Most Holy Place, and begin his Investigative Judgment of mankind.

As for legalism, Adventists advocate a conservative form of dress, restricted entertainment activities, opposition to body piercing and tattoos, and limits on the wearing of jewelry.

Adventists emphasize wholeness and health, advocating vegetarianism. John Kellogg, an Adventist, was a major leader in health reform and temperance. Consequently, he developed a breakfast cereal product known as Corn Flakes which resulted in a lasting change of the American breakfast.

For those Adventists who insist on eating meat, they are encouraged to adhere to kosher laws as described in the Eleventh chapter of Leviticus, meaning abstinence from pork, shellfish, and other animals considered to be unclean.

Church members are also discouraged from consuming alcoholic beverages, and from using tobacco.

Salvation Army

Overview. The Salvation Army is a Protestant Christian church and international charitable organization, reporting a worldwide membership of over 1.7 million, consisting of soldiers, officers and members collectively known as Salvationists. Its founders sought to bring Salvation to the poor, destitute, and hungry by meeting both their "physical and spiritual needs." It is present in 132 countries, running charity shops, operating shelters for the homeless, disaster relief, and humanitarian aid to developing countries. The Army's purpose is the advancement of the Christian religion, the relief of poverty, and other charitable objects beneficial to society or the community of mankind as a whole.

The theology of the Salvation Army is derived primarily from Methodist beliefs. One distinctive characteristic of the Salvation Army is its use of titles derived from military ranks, such as "lieutenant" or "major."

History. The Army was founded in 1865 in London by one-time Methodist preacher William Booth and his wife Catherine, as the East London Christian Mission which was later renamed, "The Salvation Army." Booth and the other members of "God's Army" would wear the Army's own uniform for meetings and ministry work. He became the General, and his other ministers were given appropriate ranks as officers. Other members became "soldiers."

Booth's early motivation for The Salvation Army was to convert poor London residents such as prostitutes, gamblers and alcoholics to Christianity, while Catherine spoke to the wealthier people, gaining financial support for their work. Booth described the organization's approach to caring for the "down and outs," known as the three "S's," which are soup, soap, and Salvation.

In 1880, the Salvation Army expanded to three other countries: Australia, Ireland, and the United States. The Salvation Army's main converts were at first alcoholics, morphine addicts, prostitutes and other "undesirables" unwelcome in polite Christian society, which helped prompt the Booths to start their own church.

As the Salvation Army grew in the late 19th century, it generated opposition in England. Opponents attacked Salvation Army meetings and gatherings with tactics such as throwing rocks, bones, rats, and tar as well as physical assaults on members of the Salvation Army. Much of this was initiated by pub owners who were losing business because of the Army's opposition to alcohol, along with the targeting of the frequenters of saloons and public houses.

The Salvation Army's reputation in the United States improved as a result of its disaster relief efforts following the Galveston Hurricane of 1900, and the 1906 San Francisco earthquake. The familiar use of bell ringers to solicit donations from passers-by helps complete the American Christmas scene. In the U.S. alone, thousands of volunteers with red kettles are stationed near retail stores during the weeks preceding Christmas for fundraising.

The Salvation Army is well known for its network of thrift stores, which raise money for its rehabilitation programs, emergency relief efforts, and other programs, by selling donated used items such as clothing, housewares and toys.

Beliefs. The Salvation Army's ministry is motivated by the love of God. Its mission is to preach the Gospel of Jesus Christ and to meet human needs in his name without discrimination. They believe the Scriptures of the Old and New Testaments were given by inspiration of God, and only they, constitute the Divine rule of Christian faith and practice. They believe there is only one God, and there are three persons in the Godhead – the Father, the Son and the Holy Ghost – undivided in essence and co-equal in power and glory. They believe that in the person of Jesus Christ, the Divine and human natures are united, so that He is truly and properly God and truly and properly man. They believe that repentance towards God, faith in our Lord Jesus Christ, and regeneration by the Holy Spirit, are necessary to salvation.

The Salvation Army does not celebrate the rites of Baptism and Holy Communion, believing that many Christians had come to rely on the outward signs of spiritual grace rather than on grace itself. However, the Army's doctrine is otherwise typical of holiness churches. Other beliefs are that its members should completely refrain from drinking alcohol, smoking, taking illegal drugs and gambling. The Salvation Army opposes euthanasia and assisted suicide. As for abortion, the Salvation

Army believes in the sanctity of all human life and considers each person to be of infinite value and each life a gift from God to be cherished, nurtured and redeemed. Human life is sacred because it is made in the image of God and has an eternal destiny. The Salvation Army teaches that homosexual practice is, in the light of Scripture, clearly unacceptable. Such activity is chosen behavior and is thus a matter of the will. It is therefore able to be directed or restrained in the same way heterosexual urges are controlled.

Church Services. The service often begins with a greeting from the Minister. Then, hymns are sung, a Scripture is read from the Bible, and prayers are led by the minister. A sermon is given, and finally, the service concludes with a benediction.

Jehovah's Witnesses

History. In 1870, Charles Taze Russell and others formed a group in Pittsburgh, Pennsylvania to study the Bible. During the course of his ministry, Russell disputed many beliefs of mainstream Christianity including immortality of the soul, hellfire, predestination, the fleshly return of Jesus Christ, the Trinity, and the burning up of the world. In 1876, Russell met Nelson H Barbour. Later that year they jointly produced the book Three Worlds, which combined restitutionist views with end time prophecy. The book taught that God's dealings with humanity were divided dispensationally, each ending with a "harvest," that Christ had returned as an invisible spirit being in 1874 inaugurating the "harvest of the Gospel age, and that 1914 would mark the end of a 2520-year period called "the Gentile Times," at which time world society would be replaced by the full establishment of God's kingdom on earth. Beginning in 1878, Russell and Barbour jointly edited a religious journal, *Herald of the Morning*. In June 1879, the two split over doctrinal differences, and in July, Russell began publishing the magazine Zion's Watch Tower and Herald of Christ's Presence, stating that its purpose was to demonstrate that the world was in "the last days," and that a new age of earthly and human restitution under the reign of Christ was imminent.

From 1879, *Watch Tower* supporters gathered as autonomous congregations to study the Bible topically. Thirty congregations were founded, and during 1879 and 1880, Russell visited each to provide the format he recommended for conducting meetings. In 1881, *Zion's Watch Tower Tract Society* was presided over by William Henry Conley, and in 1884, Russell incorporated the society as a non-profit business to distribute tracts and Bibles. By about 1900, Russell had organized thousands of part-time and full-time colporteurs, and was appointing foreign missionaries and establishing branch offices. By the 1910s, Russell's organization maintained nearly a hundred "pilgrims," or traveling preachers. Russell engaged in significant global publishing efforts during his ministry, and by 1912, he was the most distributed Christian author in the United States.

Russell moved the Watch Tower Society's headquarters to Brooklyn, New York in 1909, combining printing and corporate offices with a house of worship. Volunteers were housed in a nearby residence he named *Bethel*. He identified the religious movement as "Bible Students," and more formally as the International Bible Students Association. By 1910, about 50,000 people worldwide were associated with the movement and congregations re-elected him annually as their "pastor." Russell died October 31, 1916, at the age of 64 while returning from a ministerial speaking tour.

In January 1917, the Watch Tower Society's legal representative, Joseph Franklin Rutherford, was elected as its next president. His election was disputed, and members of the Board of Directors accused him of acting in an autocratic and secretive manner. The divisions between his supporters and opponents triggered a major turnover of members over the next decade. In June 1917, he released *The Finished Mystery* as a seventh volume of Russell's Studies in the Scriptures series. The book, published as the posthumous work of Russell, was a compilation of his commentaries on the Bible books of Ezekiel and Revelation, plus numerous additions by Bible Students Clayton Woodworth and George Fisher. It strongly criticized Catholic and Protestant clergy and Christian involvement in the Great War As a result, Watch Tower Society directors were jailed for sedition under the Espionage Act in 1918 and members were subjected to mob violence. The directors were released in March 1919 and charges against them were dropped in 1920.

Rutherford centralized organizational control of the Watch Tower Society. In 1919, he instituted the appointment of a director in each congregation, and a year later all members were instructed to report their weekly preaching activity to the Brooklyn headquarters. At an international convention held at Cedar Point, Ohio in September 1922, a new emphasis was made on house-to-house preaching. Significant changes in doctrine and administration were regularly introduced during Rutherford's twenty-five years as president, including the 1920 announcement that the Hebrew patriarchs (such as Abraham and Isaac) would be resurrected in 1925, marking the beginning of Christ's thousand-year earthly Kingdom. Because of disappointment over the changes and unfulfilled predictions, tens of thousands of defections occurred during the first half of Rutherford's tenure, leading to the formation of several Bible Student organizations independent of the Watch Tower Society, most of which still exist. By mid-1919, as many as one in seven of Russell-era Bible Students had ceased their association with the Society, and as many as three-quarters by the end of the 1920s.

On July 26, 1931, at a convention in Columbus, Ohio, Rutherford introduced the new name –*Jehovah's Witnesses*– based on Isaiah 43:10: "Ye are my witnesses, saith the Lord, and my servant whom I have chosen: that ye may know and believe me, and understand that I am he: before me there was no God formed, neither shall there be after me," which was adopted by resolution. The name was chosen to distinguish his group of Bible Students from other independent groups that had severed ties with the Society, as well as symbolize the instigation of new outlooks and the promotion of fresh evangelizing methods. In 1932, Rutherford eliminated the system of locally elected elders and in 1938, introduced what he called a "theocratic" (literally, *God-ruled*) organizational system, under which appointments in congregations worldwide were made from the Brooklyn headquarters.

From 1932, it was taught that the "little flock" of 144,000 would not be the only people to survive Armageddon. Rutherford explained that in addition to the 144,000 "anointed" who would be resurrected—or transferred at death—to live in heaven to rule over earth with Christ, a separate class of members, the "great multitude," would live in a paradise restored on earth. From 1935, new converts to the movement were considered part of that class. By the mid-1930s, the timing of the beginning of Christ's presence, his enthronement as king, and the start of the "last days" were each moved to 1914.

As their interpretations of the Bible evolved, Witness publications decreed that saluting national flags is a form of idolatry, which led to a new outbreak of mob violence and government opposition in the United States, Canada, Germany, and other countries.

Nathan Knorr was appointed as third president of the Watch Tower Bible and Tract Society in 1942. Knorr commissioned a new translation of the Bible, the New World Translation of the Holy Scriptures, the full version of which was released in 1961. He organized large international assemblies, instituted new training programs for members, and expanded missionary activity and branch offices throughout the world. Knorr's presidency was also marked by an increasing use of explicit instructions guiding Witnesses in their lifestyle and conduct, and a greater use of congregational judicial procedures to enforce a strict moral code.

From 1966, Witness publications and convention talks built anticipation of the possibility that Christ's thousand-year reign might begin in late 1975 or shortly thereafter. The number of baptisms increased significantly, from about 59,000 in 1966 to more than 297,000 in 1974. By 1975, the number of active members exceeded two million. Membership declined during the late 1970s after expectations for 1975 were proved wrong. Watch Tower Society literature did not state dogmatically that 1975 would definitely mark the end, but in 1980 the Watch Tower Society admitted its responsibility in building up hope regarding that year.

The offices of elder and ministerial servant were restored to Witness congregations in 1972, with appointments made from headquarters, and later, also by branch committees. It was announced that, starting in September 2014, appointments would be made by traveling overseers. In a major organizational overhaul in 1976, the power of the Watch Tower Society president was diminished, with authority for doctrinal and organizational decisions passed to the Governing Body Since Knorr's death in 1977, the position of president has been occupied by Frederick Franz (1977–1992) and Milton Henschel (1992–2000), both members of the Governing Body, and since 2000 by others who are not Governing Body members. In 1995, Jehovah's Witnesses abandoned the idea that Armageddon must occur during the lives of the generation that was alive in 1914 and in 2010 changed their teaching on the "generation."

Beliefs. Baptism is a requirement for being considered a member of Jehovah's Witnesses. Jehovah's Witnesses do not practice infant baptism, and previous baptisms performed by other denominations are not considered valid. Individuals undergoing baptism must affirm publicly that dedication and baptism identify them as one of Jehovah's Witnesses in association with God's spirit-directed organization, though Witness publications say baptism symbolizes personal dedication to God and not to a man, work or organization. Their literature emphasizes the need for members to be obedient and loyal to Jehovah and to his organization, stating that individuals must remain part of it to receive God's favor and to survive Armageddon.

Jehovah's Witnesses believe their denomination is a restoration of first-century Doctrines of Jehovah's Witnesses. They are established by the Governing Body, which assumes responsibility for interpreting and applying scripture. The Governing Body does not issue any single, comprehensive statement of faith, but prefers to express its doctrinal position in a variety of ways through publications published by the Watch Tower Society. Their publications teach that doctrinal changes and refinements result from a process of progressive revelation, in which God gradually reveals his will and purpose, and that such enlightenment, or new light, results from the application of reason and study, the guidance of the holy spirit, and direction from Jesus Christ and angels. The Society also teaches that members of the Governing Body are helped by the holy spirit to discern deep truths, which are then considered by the entire Governing Body before it makes doctrinal decisions. The group's leadership, while disclaiming divine inspiration and infallibility, is said to provide divine guidance through its teachings described as, "based on God's Word thus, not from men, but from Jehovah."

The entire Protestant canon of Scripture is considered the inspired, inerrant Word of God. Jehovah's Witnesses consider the Bible to be scientifically and historically accurate and reliable and interpret much of it literally, but accept parts of it as symbolic. They consider the Bible to be the final authority for all their beliefs. Regular personal Bible reading is frequently recommended; Witnesses are discouraged from formulating doctrines and "private ideas" reached through Bible research independent of Watch Tower Society publications, and are cautioned against reading other religious literature. Adherents are told to have complete confidence in the leadership, avoid skepticism about what is taught in the Watch Tower Society's literature, and not to advocate or insist on personal opinions or harbor private ideas when it comes to Bible understanding. The organization makes no provision for members to criticize or contribute to official teachings and all Witnesses must abide by its doctrines and organizational requirements.

Jehovah's Witnesses emphasize the use of God's name, and they prefer the form Jehovah—a vocalization of God's name. They believe that Jehovah is the only true God, the creator of all things, and the, "Universal Sovereign." They believe that all worship should be directed toward him, and that he is not part of a Trinity. Consequently, the group places more emphasis on God than on Christ. They believe that the Holy Spirit is God's applied power or active force, rather than a person.

Jehovah's Witnesses believe that Jesus is God's only direct creation, that everything else was created through Christ by means of God's power, and that the initial unassisted act of creation uniquely identifies Jesus as God's only-begotten Son. Jesus served as a redeemer and a ransom sacrifice to pay for the sins of humanity. They believe Jesus died on a single upright post rather than the traditional cross. Biblical references to the Archangel Michael, Abasson, (Apollyon), and the Word are interpreted as names for Jesus in various roles. Jesus is considered to be the only intercessor and high priest between God and humanity, and appointed by God as the king and judge of his kingdom. His role as a mediator, referred to in 1 Timothy 2:5, is applied to the "anointed" class, though the "other sheep," are said to also benefit from the arrangement.

Jehovah's Witnesses believe that Satan was originally a perfect angel who developed feelings of self-importance and craved worship. Satan influenced Adam and Eve to disobey God, and humanity subsequently became participants in a challenge involving the competing claims of Jehovah and Satan to universal sovereignty. Other angels who sided with Satan became demons.

Jehovah's Witnesses teach that Satan and his demons were cast down to earth from heaven after October 1, 1914, at which point the end times began. They believe that Satan is the ruler of the current world order, that human society is influenced and misled by Satan and his demons, and that they are a cause of human suffering. They also believe that human governments are controlled by Satan, but that he does not directly control each human ruler.

Jehovah's Witnesses believe death is a state of non-existence with no consciousness. There is no Hell of fiery torment. Hades and Sheol are understood to refer to the condition of death, termed the *common grave*. Jehovah's Witnesses consider the soul to be a life or a living body that can die. Jehovah's Witnesses believe that humanity is in a sinful state, from which release is only possible by means of Jesus' shed blood as a ransom, or atonement, for the sins of humankind.

Witnesses believe that a "little flock" of 144,000 selected humans go to heaven, but that the majority, the other sheep, are to be resurrected by God to a cleansed earth after Armageddon. They interpret Revelation 14:1–5 to mean that the number of Christians going to heaven is limited to exactly 144,000, who will rule with Jesus as kings and priests over earth. They believe that baptism as a Jehovah's Witness is vital for salvation and that only they meet scriptural requirements for surviving Armageddon, but that God is the final judge. During Christ's millennial reign, most people who died prior to Armageddon will be resurrected with the prospect of living forever. They will be taught the proper way to worship God to prepare them for their final test at the end of the millennium.

Jehovah's Witnesses believe that God's Kingdom is a literal government in heaven, ruled by Jesus Christ and 144,000 "spirit-anointed" Christians drawn from the earth, which they associate with Jesus' reference to a new covenant. The kingdom is viewed as the means by which God will accomplish his original purpose for the earth, transforming it into a paradise without sickness or death. It is said to have been the focal point of Jesus' ministry on earth. They believe the kingdom was established in heaven in 1914, and that Jehovah's Witnesses serve as representatives of the kingdom on earth.

A central teaching of Jehovah's Witnesses is that the current world era, or system of things, entered the last days in 1914 and faces imminent destruction through intervention by God and Jesus Christ, leading to deliverance for those who worship God acceptably. They consider all other present-day religions to be false, identifying them with "Babylon the Great," or the "harlot," of Revelation 17, and believe that they will soon be destroyed by the United Nations, which they believe is represented in scripture by the scarlet-colored wild beast of Revelation, Chapter 17. This development will mark the beginning of the "great tribulation." Satan will subsequently use world governments to attack Jehovah's Witnesses, an action that will prompt God to begin the war of Armageddon, during which all forms of government and all people not counted as Christ's sheep will be destroyed. After Armageddon, God will extend his heavenly kingdom to include earth, which will be transformed into a paradise similar to the Garden of Eden. Most of those who had died before God's intervention will gradually be resurrected during the thousand-year judgment day. This judgment will be based on their actions after resurrection rather than past deeds. At the end of the thousand years, Christ will hand all authority back to God. Then a final test will take place when Satan is released to mislead perfect mankind. Those who fail will be destroyed, along with Satan and his demons. The result will be a fully tested, glorified human race on earth.

Jehovah's Witnesses believe that Jesus Christ began to rule in heaven as king of God's kingdom in October 1914, and that Satan was subsequently ousted from heaven to earth, resulting in woe to humanity. They believe that Jesus rules invisibly, from heaven, perceived only as a series of signs. They base this belief on a rendering of the Greek word parsousia—usually translated as, "coming" when referring to Christ, as "presence," instead. They believe Jesus' presence includes an unknown period beginning with his inauguration as king in heaven in 1914, and ending when he comes to bring a final judgment against humans on earth. They thus depart from the mainstream Christian belief that the second coming of Matthew 24 refers to a single moment of arrival on earth to judge humans.

All sexual relations outside of marriage are grounds for expulsion if the individual is not deemed repentant. Homosexual activity is considered a serious sin, and same-sex marriages are forbidden. Abortion is considered murder. Suicide is considered to be self-murder, and a sin against God. Modesty in dress and grooming is frequently emphasized. Gambling, drunkenness, illegal drugs, and tobacco use are forbidden. Drinking of alcoholic beverages is permitted in moderation.

The family structure is patriarchal. The husband is considered to have authority on family decisions, but is encouraged to solicit his wife's thoughts and feelings, as well as those of his children. Marriages are required to be monogamous and legally registered. Marrying a non-believer, or endorsing such a union, is strongly discouraged and carries religious sanctions.

Divorce is discouraged, and remarriage is forbidden unless a divorce is obtained on the grounds of adultery, which they refer to as a scriptural divorce. If a divorce is obtained for any other reason, remarriage is considered adulterous unless the prior spouse has died or is since considered to have committed sexual immorality. Extreme physical abuse, willful non-support of one's family, and what the denomination terms, "absolute endangerment of spirituality" are accepted as grounds for legal separation.

Jehovah's Witnesses believe that only Jehovah's Witnesses represent true Christianity, and that other religions fail to meet all the requirements set by God and will soon be destroyed. Jehovah's Witnesses are taught that it is vital to remain separate from the world. The Witnesses' literature defines the world as the mass of mankind apart from Jehovah's approved servants, and teach that it is morally contaminated and ruled by Satan. Witnesses are taught that association with worldly people presents a danger to their faith, and are instructed to minimize social contact with non-members to better maintain their own standards of morality. Attending a university is discouraged and trade schools are suggested as an alternative.

Although they do not take part in politics, they respect the authority of the governments under which they live. They do not celebrate religious holidays such as Christmas and Easter, nor do they observe birthdays, national holidays, or other celebrations they consider to honor people other than Jesus. They feel that these and many other customs have pagan origins or reflect a nationalistic or political spirit. Their position is that these traditional holidays reflect Satan's control over the world. Witnesses are told that spontaneous giving at other times can help their children to not feel deprived of birthdays or other celebrations.

They do not work in industries associated with the military, do not serve in the armed services, and refuse national military service, which in some countries may result in their arrest and imprisonment. They do not salute or pledge allegiance to flags or sing national anthems or patriotic songs. Jehovah's Witnesses see themselves as a worldwide brotherhood that transcends national boundaries and ethnic loyalties.

Worship. Meetings for worship and study are held at Kingdom Halls, which are typically functional in character, and do not contain religious symbols. Witnesses are assigned to a congregation in whose territory they usually reside and attend weekly services they refer to as, "meetings" as scheduled by congregation elders. The meetings are largely devoted to study of Watch Tower Society literature and the Bible. The format of the meetings is established by the group's headquarters, and the subject matter for most meetings is the same worldwide. Congregations meet for two sessions each week comprising four distinct meetings that total about three-and-a-half hours, typically gathering mid-week (two meetings) and on the weekend (two meetings). Prior to 2009, congregations met three times each week; these meetings were condensed, with the intention that members dedicate an evening for "family worship." Gatherings are opened and closed with hymns (which they call Kingdom songs) and brief prayers. Twice each year, Witnesses from a number of congregations that form a, "circuit," gather for a one-day assembly. Larger groups of congregations meet once a year for a three-day regional convention, usually at rented stadiums or auditoriums. Their most important and solemn event is the commemoration of the "Lord's Evening Meal," or "Memorial of Christ's Death," on the date of the Jewish Passover.

Evangelism. Jehovah's Witnesses are known for their efforts to spread their beliefs, most notably by visiting people from house to house, and distributing literature published by the Watch Tower Society. The objective is to start a regular Bible study with any person who is not already a member, with the intention that the student be baptized as a member of the group. Witnesses are advised to consider discontinuing Bible studies with students who show no interest in becoming members. Witnesses are taught they are under a biblical command to engage in public preaching. They are instructed to devote as much time as possible to their ministry and are required to submit an individual monthly "Field Service Report." Baptized members who fail to report a month of preaching are termed, "irregular" and may be counseled by elders. Those who do not submit reports for six consecutive months are termed, "inactive."

Church of Christ Scientist

Beginnings. Christian Science was founded by Mary Baker Eddy, who argued in her 1875 book, "Science and Health with Key to the Scriptures" that sickness is nothing but an illusion that can be corrected by prayer alone. Eddy's book became Christian Science's central text, along with the Bible. In 1879, with the support of 26 followers, Eddy founded the Church of Christ Scientist.

Eddy described her newly formed Christian Science as a return to "primitive Christianity and its lost element of healing." According to Christian Science theology, disease is a mental error, rather than physical disorder, and those who are sick should not be treated by medicine, but by a form of prayer that seeks to correct the beliefs responsible for the illusion of ill health. The church doesn't require its members to avoid all medical care. They use dentists, optometrists, obstetricians, physicians for broken bones, and vaccinations when required by law. Nevertheless, the church maintains that prayer is most effective when not combined with medicine. Christian

Scientists avoid almost all medical treatment, relying instead on Christian Science prayer. This consists of silently arguing with oneself. There are no appeals to a personal god, and no set words.

Christian Science became known as a "mind-cure" movement because of its strong focus on healing. Medical practice was in its infancy at that time, and patients typically fared better without it. This provided fertile soil for the mind-cure groups, who argued that sickness was an absence of "right thinking" or failure to connect to Divine Mind. Eddy also promoted the concept of "malicious animal magnetism," which is the belief that people can be harmed by the bad thoughts of others. She dismissed the material world as an illusion, leading her to reject the use of medicine.

Theology and Healing Practices. Christian Science theology differs in several respects from that of traditional mainstream Christianity, including the Trinity, divinity of Jesus, atonement, and resurrection. At the core of Eddy's theology is the view that the spiritual world is the only reality, and is entirely good, and that the material world, with its evil, sickness and death, is nothing more than an illusion.

Church Services. The Church of Christ, Scientist has no ordained clergy or rituals, and performs no baptisms. Typically, clergy of other faiths will perform marriage or funeral services. The main religious texts of the church consist of the Bible and Eddy's "Science and Health." Each church has two Readers, who read aloud a "Bible lesson" or "lesson sermon" made up of selections from those texts during the Sunday service. During the Wednesday meetings, there are shorter readings, supplemented by members offering testimonials, including recovery from ill health attributed to prayer. There are also hymns, time for silent prayer, and repeating together the Lord's Prayer at each service.

Church of the Nazarene

The Church of the Nazarene is a Christian denomination that emerged from a series of mergers that occurred between various holiness churches and denominations. The First General Assembly held in Chicago in 1907, brought together the Eastern and the Western Wesleyan Holiness streams. The Western group was the Church of the Nazarene which had been founded in 1895 by Dr. Phineas F. Bresee, a minister in the Methodist Episcopal Church, and Dr. Joseph Promeroy Widney, a Methodist physician.

The name, "Nazarene" comes from the biblical description of Jesus Christ, who had been raised in the village of Nazareth, and consequently regarded as a Nazarene. The denomination started out as a church that ministered to the homeless and poor, and wanted to keep that attitude of ministering to "lower classes" of society.

The Nazarene affirmations include justification by grace through faith alone in Jesus Christ, sanctification by grace through faith and united with good works, entire sanctification as an inheritance available to every Christian, and the witness of the Spirit to God's work in human lives. The holiness movement arose in the 1830s to promote these doctrines, especially Entire Sanctification, but splintered by 1900. The Church of the Nazarene remains committed to Christian holiness.

For Wesley, the founder of Wesleyanism, good works were the fruit of one's salvation, not the way in which that Salvation was earned. Faith and good works go hand in hand in Methodist theology—a living tree naturally and inevitably bears fruit. Unlike many Baptists and some others, Wesleyan theology rejects the Doctrine of Eternal Security, believing Salvation can be rejected. Wesley emphasized that believers must continue to grow in their relationship with Christ, through the process of Sanctification.

The Church of the Nazarene also takes a stance on a variety of moral and social issues. These issues include human sexuality, theatrical arts, movies, social dancing, AIDS/HIV, and organ donation. On some matters, such as human sexuality, the church is very conservative and stipulates that homosexuality is a sin that is subject to the wrath of God.

Throughout its history, the Church of the Nazarene has maintained a stance supporting abstinence from alcohol and cigarettes. While the church does not consider alcohol itself to be the cause of sin, it recognizes that intoxication is a danger to many people, both physically and spiritually. Historically, the Nazarene Church was founded in order to help the poor. Alcohol, gambling, and their addictions, were cited as things that kept people poor. So in order to help the poor, as well as everyone else, Nazarenes have traditionally abstained from those things. Also, a person who is meant to serve as an example to others should avoid the use of them, in order not to cause others to stray from their walk with God, as that is considered a sin for both parties.

While Nazarenes believe that those who are sick should utilize all appropriate medical opportunities, they also affirm God's will of divine healing, and pastors may lay hands on the ill in prayer, either at the hospital, or in a worship service. A prayer for divine healing is never understood as excluding medical services and agencies.

Church of Christ

History. The Churches of Christ arose as the result of a division within the Christian Church (Disciples of Christ). This division, which began in 1860, was centered around the usage of musical instruments in worship. Certain groups within the Disciples of Christ protested the usage of musical instruments because none were found to have been used in the New Testament Church. To them, any practices not found in the accounts of the New Testament Church should not be permitted in the modern-day Church. At long last, the U.S. Religious Census in 1906 listed the Church of Christ as a separate and distinct church.

The Church of Christ did not view itself as having its roots in the 19th century. Rather, they claimed to be the Church which was established on the Day of Pentecost in 33 A.D. They sought to base their doctrines and practices on the Bible alone, rather than recognizing the traditional councils of men that had come to define Christianity after the close of the New Testament. They declared that Jesus Christ founded the one and only

Church, and that the current divisions among Christians do not express God's Will.

Beliefs. Churches of Christ generally refuse to adopt any formal creeds, doctrinal statements, or statements of faith. They baptize by way of immersion, observe the Lord's Supper each Sunday, and practice a cappella singing in worship services. The Church of Christ generally teaches that Salvation involves, faith, repentance, confession that Jesus is the Son of God, baptism, and living faithfully as a Christian. As time goes on however, may preachers place more emphasis on Grace in Salvation rather than focusing on implementing all of the New Testament commands and examples.

Church of God

History. Baptist minister, R.G. Spurling, and his father, Richard expressed objections to the Baptist view that only churches with the Baptist doctrine were part of the true Church. When this objection was voiced, they were barred from the local church in 1886, which resulted in Spurling and eight others organizing a church that stood on the principles of the New Testament. They agreed to free themselves from man-made creeds, and unite upon the principles of the New Testament.

Between 1889 and 1895, Spurling organized three other congregations, all with the name Christian Union. Between 1889 and 1895, Spurling organized three other congregations, all with the name Christian Union, each functioning independently under Baptist polity. While this group would later disband and its members return to their original churches, the Church of God traces its origins to this 1886 meeting.

In 1896, three Tennessee evangelists (William Martin, Joe M. Tipton, and Milton McNabb) with links to Benjamin H.

Irwin's Fire-Baptized Holiness Church, brought the message of entire sanctification to the western North Carolina countryside. A feature of this revival was that some participants, including children, spoke in tongues when they experienced sanctification (this was later understood to be the baptism of the Holy Ghost, as spoken of in Acts 2). This phenomenon caused great excitement and controversy in the community, and leading Baptist and Methodist leaders soon denounced the revival. Several of the worshiper's homes, as well as a provisional meeting house were burned by mobs opposing the new revival.

The worshipers began to meet in the house of William F. Bryant (1863–1949), a Baptist deacon prior to his joining the holiness movement, who assumed leadership of the group. R.G. Spurling often worshiped with the small fellowship and was the driving force behind its 1902 decision to organize into a church, called the Holiness Church at Camp Creek. Organization was made necessary because Irwin's more fanatical teachings were influencing the movement, and there was a need for authority to discipline erring members.

It would be A. J. Tomlinson and his organizational skills, however, that would be responsible for the growth of the Camp Creek Holiness Church into a national denomination.

Tomlinson had received the sanctification experience but had not spoken in tongues. In 1903, Tomlinson joined the church and was soon elected its pastor. This allowed Spurling and Bryant to pursue evangelism. Fourteen new members were added to the church in the first year of Tomlinson's pastorate, and other churches were soon established in Georgia and Tennessee.

By 1905, there was a desire for greater organization among the churches. Delegates from four churches met at Camp Creek (approximately a mile northwest of Fields of the Wood) in January 1906 to conduct the 1st General Assembly of the "Churches of East Tennessee, North Georgia, and Western North Carolina." Though the intention was still to avoid the creation of a creed and denomination, the members' consensus on certain endeavors and standards laid the groundwork for the future denomination. The Assembly declared, "We hope and trust that no person or body of people will ever use these minutes, or any part of them, as articles of faith upon which to establish a sect or denomination," and that the General Assembly was not a legislative or executive body, but judicial only. The 1st Assembly decided that foot washing was on the same level as the sacrament of communion and, like other holiness groups, condemned the use of tobacco. Tomlinson served as moderator and secretary. The name "Church of God" was adopted in 1907, and Tomlinson was elected general overseer in 1909.

The Church of God was a part of the holiness movement and believed in entire sanctification as a definite experience occurring after salvation. While individuals had spoken in tongues in the 1896 revival, tongues were not yet understood by the Church of God to be the initial evidence of baptism in the Holy Spirit. As news of the Azusa Street Revival began to spread and reach the Southeast, Church of God adherents began to seek and obtain Spirit baptism. Tomlinson was one of these seekers. In June 1907, he traveled to Birmingham, Alabama, to attend a meeting of M.M. Pinson and Gaston B. Cashwell. After being baptized in the Spirit at Azusa Street, Cashwell had returned to the South, spreading the revival and bringing many holiness groups into the Pentecostal fold. Tomlinson invited Cashwell to preach in Cleveland, Tennessee. It was there, under Cashwell's preaching, that Tomlinson received the Pentecostal blessing. After Tomlinson's experience, the Church of God's emphasis changed from being mainly holiness in nature, to being both holiness and Pentecostal, and it has identified that way ever since.

In 1910, the official publication, "The Church of God Evangel," was founded, and it remains the oldest continuous Pentecostal publication.

Assemblies of God

Overview. The Assemblies originated from the Azusa Street Revival of the early 20th century. This revival led to the founding, in 1914, of the Assemblies of God. Established churches generally did not welcome the Pentecostal aspects of the revival, and participants in the new movement soon found themselves forced outside existing religious bodies. These people sought out their own places of worship and founded hundreds of distinctly Pentecostal congregations. By 1914 many ministers and laymen alike began to realize just how far-reaching the spread of the revival and of Pentecostalism had become. Through foreign missionary work and establishing relationships with other Pentecostal churches, the Assemblies of God expanded into a worldwide movement.

History. Even though there were rare and scattered reports of tongues in the 1800's, the resumption of the outpouring of the Holy Ghost in the modern era has been officially traced to Topeka, Kansas in 1901. Just a few years later, the focal point of the Holy Ghost revival moved from Topeka to Azusa Street in Los Angeles.

Today, a number of charismatic denominations refer to Topeka, Kansas and Azusa Street as the beginning point of their particular beliefs, and one of those denominations is the Assemblies of God (AG). It was Durham's Finished Work theology of gradual progressive sanctification, which he announced in 1910, that was to become a significant catalyst that resulted in the formation of the Assemblies of God in 1914.

Shortly after his break with Parham, Howard Goss and his first wife, Millicent, began preaching revivals around Texas, and then they moved to Arkansas, which became the center of the Apostolic Faith group that was once overseen by Parham. It was here in Arkansas that these believers began referring to themselves as Pentecostals rather than the "Apostolic Faith Group." This was partly, if not wholly, done in an effort to disaffiliate themselves with controversial scandals associated with Parham.

In 1909, while attending a camp meeting in Houston, Texas, Goss met Eudorus Neander Bell (E.N. Bell), a former Baptist pastor from Fort Worth who had recently been drawn to the new doctrine of Pentecostalism. These two new friends would soon be the men credited with the formation of the Assemblies of God.

After accepting Durham's Finished Work doctrine, Goss moved even further from Parham. He wrote that God revealed to him that the Plan of Salvation was truly finished on the cross. It didn't take long for him to realize that the attempted measures for cooperation between ministers and churches that had developed after the collapse of Parham's Apostolic Faith movement in 1907 were not working. Consequently, Goss and many of the remnants of the Apostolic Faith group joined the Church of God in Christ (COGIC).

This alliance with the COGIC didn't last long. Even though Goss had received credentials in the Church of God in Christ, he continued to nurture a growing dissatisfaction with the arrangement. Goss and several other leaders felt that the organization was lacking in missionary solidarity and protection of local churches. According to Goss' way of thinking, this perceived deficiency demanded a more definite organizational tie between various Pentecostal groups across the country. Consequently, plans began to formulate in his mind for the development of a different kind of Pentecostal organization.

Goss was poised to be instrumental in playing a key role in organizing the Finished Work adherents into a new organization that would be called the Assemblies of God. Late in the fall of 1913, while serving as pastor in Hot Springs, Arkansas, Goss discussed the matter at length with E.N. Bell, who was the editor of the publication known as the, "Word and Witness." Goss was already leasing the Grand Opera House in Hot Springs, so the two men decided to issue a call for a General Council to meet there on April 2–12, 1914. Carried on the front page of the December 20, 1913, issue of *Word and Witness*, an article was addressed to "The Pentecostal Saints and Churches of God in Christ."

The article in the Word and Witness called for the independent churches to band together for the purposes of fellowship and doctrinal unity. The title of the article was, "General Convention of Pentecostal Saints and Churches of God in Christ." The beginning of the article read, "We desire at this time to make this preliminary announcement of this general meeting, so that workers far and near, at home and abroad, may sidetrack everything else, and be present. Laymen as well as preachers are invited. Especially do we urge all elders, pastors, ministers, evangelists and missionaries to be present. This call is to all the Churches of God in Christ, to all Pentecostal or Apostolic Faith assemblies who desire with united purpose to co-operate in love and peace to push the interests of the kingdom of God everywhere. This is, however, only for saints who believe in the baptism of the Holy Ghost with the signs following."

There were other concerns on Goss' agenda. He wanted to facilitate mission work, charter churches, and form a Bible training school. The first meeting was held in Hot Springs, Arkansas, in April 1914. About 300 church leaders showed up at the meeting. After three days of prayer and preaching, the business at hand was discussed. Apprehensive about creating another denomination, those attending agreed to form a loosely knit fellowship of independent churches. So began the General Council of the Assemblies of God.

By a motion from the floor, 12 men became members of the Executive Presbytery. Two of those elected members were E.N. Bell and H.A. Goss. Bell became the first General Superintendent of the Assemblies of God, and Howard A. Goss was appointed to be a member of the Executive Board.

The Assemblies of God was birthed in the fires of revival that swept the world at the turn of the century. The participants in the revival claimed to be filled with the Holy Spirit in a fashion similar to that of the disciples and followers of Jesus Christ. Therefore, the participants of this latter-day revival called themselves, "Pentecostal." The Assemblies of God would go on to become the largest Pentecostal organization in the world.

Beliefs. As a Pentecostal fellowship, the Assemblies of God believes in the Pentecostal distinction of baptism with the Holy Spirit with the evidence of speaking in tongues. The AG teaches that this experience is distinct from and subsequent to the experience of Salvation. The baptism in the Holy Spirit empowers the believer for Christian life and service. The initial evidence of the baptism in the Holy Spirit is speaking in tongues as the Spirit gives utterance (Acts 2:4), It also believes in the present-day use of other spiritual gifts such as divine healing.

United Pentecostal Church International

The New Issue. About the same time Howard Goss was convincing Pentecostal believers to unite under the umbrella of the Assemblies of God, a new Pentecostal belief was formulating. This new belief had to do with a different viewpoint regarding the makeup of the Godhead, along with a different opinion on the requirements for attaining salvation. This emerging belief would eventually become known as the "New Issue."

This "New Issue" would evolve into what is now referred to as the Oneness doctrine. When studying the formation and rise of the "New Issue," it would be a good idea to view it from the perspective of today's Oneness doctrine. While there were a few isolated historical figures in ages past who had written about the Oneness of the Godhead, there doesn't appear to be a similar historical thread regarding the Oneness' requirement of being baptized in Jesus Name. Likewise, there doesn't appear to by any historical thread having to do with the requirement of receiving the Holy Ghost with the evidence of speaking in other tongues.

Starting in 1901, Pentecostalism was all about the latter day outpouring of the Holy Ghost. A short time later, Durham's "Finished Work" began shaking up the fledgling Pentecostal movement. Then, in the second decade of the 20th century, the "New Issue" began to manifest itself among certain Pentecostal believers.

It was on the west coast, where these serious challenges began to rise up against the Trinitarian doctrine of the Godhead, against the Trinitarian method of baptism, and against the Trinitarian belief that Salvation occurs when a convert accepts Jesus Christ as Lord and Savior.

It is commonly believed that the New Issue got its start on April 15, 1913 at the World-Wide Apostolic Faith Camp Meeting that was being held at Arroyo Seco, California. On that day, Canadian evangelist, Robert E. McAlister, preached a sermon on baptism. The topic of his sermon had to do with the fact that the traditional formula of, "In the Name of the Father, and of the Son, and of the Holy Ghost," was not utilized by the early Church. Instead, the apostles used the formula, "In the Name of Jesus Christ," when baptizing new converts.

McAlister went so far as to claim that the traditional Trinity formula was untrue, and that baptism should always be done in the Name of Jesus Christ.

On the next morning, a man named John Scheppe was seen running through the camp grounds shouting that God had revealed to him the truth of baptism in the Name of Jesus. Shortly after that, Frank Ewart also decided to embrace McAlister's new proposition. As a result of the conversion of these trustworthy men, re-baptism presented itself not just as an option, but as a requirement before a Christian could claim Salvation. McAlister's message became known as "The New Issue," and it was from his message in 1913 that modern-day Oneness Pentecostal theology was launched.

Another big player in the Pentecostal movement was G.T. Haywood. After he accepted the premise of the New Issue doctrine, his entire congregation was converted to Jesus Name baptism. In spite of his acceptance of Jesus Name baptism however, Haywood still clung to the belief that faith in Jesus Christ was sufficient for salvation if one did not understand the water and spirit doctrine of the Oneness theology. Even as a New Issue believer, he did not regard Christians who weren't baptized in the Name of Jesus as lost. In this regard, he was still a supporter of Durham's Finished Work doctrine.

According to Durham's Finished Work theology, the very moment a sinner honestly accepts Jesus Christ as his Savior, God accepts that sinner as his child. Durham said that the work was finished by Christ, and all that humankind can, or must, do, is believe and receive. He said the doctrine of equating Spirit baptism with the new birth is false doctrine. Faith alone is what identifies one with Christ. The New Birth is a birth of faith, not of water, not of spirit, and not of works, but of divine grace received through faith.

The New Issue began evolving away from Durham's Finished Work as the new theology of the Name of Jesus Christ began to emerge. Oneness proponents explained it in this manner: "The Father is God, The Son is God, and the Holy Ghost is God. The name of this one God is the Lord Jesus Christ." Having determined that the name of God is Jesus Christ, it became even easier to conclude that the proper apostolic formula for water baptism was, "In the Name of the Lord Jesus Christ."

Just to clear up certain matters of history, Jesus Name baptism was not *entirely* the product of turn of the 20th century theology. Even though there appears to be no historical thread of Jesus Name baptism down through the centuries, there have been rare occasions in history when Jesus Name baptism has been mentioned. It's been said that at one time, Martin Luther was involved in a debate concerning the proper baptismal formula. Also, it has been reported that diverse Trinitarian groups have occasionally engaged in baptism in the Name of Jesus Christ.

Back to the turn of the 20th century, John Miller attempted to harmonize Matt. 28:19 with Acts 2:38 even though he maintained his basic Trinitarian beliefs. He said, "If it says, baptizing them in the name of the Father, the Son and the Holy Ghost, it means in the One Glorious Name, enthroned as Father, enthroned as the Son, and engrafted as the Holy Ghost. That Name is the Lord Jesus Christ." Miller was trying to explain that baptism in the titles was identical to baptism in the Name of Jesus.

William Phillips Hall agreed with John Miller by attempting to solve the apparent contradiction between Matt. 28:19 and Act 2:38. He did this by equating the titles, Father, Son and Holy Spirit with the threefold name of the Lord Jesus Christ.

The Oneness movement however, rejected the explanations of both Phillips and Miller. Additionally, the Oneness movement rejected the Trinitarian baptismal formula, along with the rest of the doctrine of the Trinity. The Oneness doctrine supported the premise that there was only one legitimate baptism, which was, "In the Name of Jesus Christ." Any other baptism formula was of none effect.

As early as 1902, Charles Parham, the man who ushered in the latter day outpouring of the Holy Ghost, had already developed some concerns regarding the proper baptismal formula. He baptized many of his converts in the Jesus Name formula, one of which, was Howard Goss. However, it wasn't until 1913 that the institution of Jesus Name baptism was put on the map by R.E. McAlister.

Andrew D. Urshan was at the California camp meeting in 1913 when McAlister preached that those in the apostolic age baptized only in the Name of Jesus. As a result of that message, he too began baptizing converts in the apostolic manner. Where he differed with the New Issue proponents however, was that for a period of time, he refused to demand that Christians be *re-baptized* in Jesus Name. Nevertheless, most of the hard-nosed proponents of the New Issue remained overtly adamant that people must be re-baptized in the Name of Jesus Christ in order to be assured of salvation.

The "New Issue" doctrine had quickly evolved to the point of insisting on re-baptism in the Name of Jesus Christ for salvation, along with a belief that Jesus was the only Person in the Godhead. This belief led to an outright denial of the orthodox doctrine of the Trinity. Oneness and Trinity had finally drifted poles apart regarding the requirements for salvation.

As a result of the New Issue, today's Oneness Pentecostals declare that the Godhead consists of only one Person and they claim that the traditional doctrine of the Trinity is a false doctrine. They maintain that the only real Person in the Godhead is Jesus. Consequently, they are typically referred to as the "Jesus Only" Movement.

Oneness Pentecostals adamantly claim that God exists as the Father in heaven, and he existed as Jesus the Son on earth. Oneness doctrine says that the Father and the Son are the same Person, not separate Persons. The Holy Spirit is not regarded as a Person at all. Instead, the Holy Spirit is merely a manifestation of Jesus' power that resides in the hearts of true believers.

The New Issue, or the Oneness Pentecostal movement, had its roots in the theological themes of Weleyanism and Durham's Finished Work. However, their denial of the doctrine of the Trinity and their requirements of being re-baptized in the Name of Jesus Christ set them apart from mainstream Christendom. The Oneness doctrine developed into a Monarchian view of the Godhead, insisting that Jesus Christ is the revealed name of God, and salvation comes by one, and only one threefold formula which is detailed in Acts 2:38. *"Then Peter said unto them, Repent, and be baptized every one of you in the name of Jesus Christ for the remission of sins, and ye shall receive the gift of the Holy Ghost."*

Trinitarian Christianity claims to embrace the Son of God who gave his life as a ransom on the cross to deliver sinners from eternal punishment, and all one has to do in order to assure salvation, is to accept Jesus into their hearts as Lord and Savior. On the other hand, the Oneness doctrine requires an exact baptismal formula, speaking in tongues, and adherence to a prescribed set of "standards" in order to merit salvation.

Oneness Controversy in the Assemblies of God. In 1914, Frank Ewart began teaching that the name of the one true God was Jesus Christ. Before long, he was busy re-baptizing a host of Pentecostals in Jesus' Name. For a short while during this period of time, E.N. Bell of the Assemblies of God was also advocating Jesus Name baptism. Parham had baptized Howard Goss in Jesus Name in 1903, but after the advent of the New Issue, Goss asked E.N. Bell to re-baptize him in the Name of Jesus at a camp meeting in Little Rock, Arkansas.

This rash of re-baptisms was destined to cause a controversy in the Assemblies of God, as its members began taking sides along these doctrinal lines. The mostly Trinitarian body feared that their organization was heading down the wrong pathway. Division eventually shook the membership to the core, with some members claiming that Jesus Name baptism was the one and only way to salvation, while others were sticking to the traditional Trinitarian baptism formula according to Matthew 28:19.

About the same time that the United States was actively involved in World War I (July 1914 to November 1918, the Assemblies of God was entangled in a different sort of battle. By the summer of 1915, the Assemblies of God was churning in turmoil over the issue of baptism in the Name of Jesus Christ. It didn't take long for the advocates of the New Issue to challenge the underlying principles of the Assemblies of God. One particularly difficult pill for the Trinitarian faction to swallow, was the insistence by the Oneness advocates that every person who had previously been baptized in the Trinitarian formula, must be re-baptized in the Name of Jesus Christ.

At the Third General Council of the Assemblies of God in October 1915, a debate took place regarding the merits of Jesus Name baptism vs. the invocation utilized by the traditional Trinitarian doctrine. At the time of this debate, a number of AG leaders had already submitted to re-baptism. Many of those leaders, such as E.N. Bell, Howard Goss, G.T. Haywood, and William T. Witherspoon, were quite prominent in the organization. Among those speaking in behalf of Jesus Name baptism were G.T. Haywood and E.N. Bell. The conference ended with no decision being made, so they opted to bring the topic up for further discussion at the Fourth General Council meeting in 1916.

The New Issue advocates didn't sit idly by during the months between the Third and Fourth Councils. In addition to pushing Jesus Name baptism, they boldly proclaimed that the Trinitarian understanding of the Godhead was completely and utterly wrong. This was when E.N. Bell drew a line in the sand and withdrew his support of the Oneness doctrine. As Bell was re-affirming the doctrine of the Trinity, Howard Goss was moving deeper into the Oneness camp.

Finally, in October, 1916, the Fourth General Council of the Assemblies of God convened. The Trinitarian faction of the organization viewed the New Issue as a heretical doctrine. Facing an opposing majority, G.T. Haywood, Howard Goss, and Frank Ewart spoke in favor of the New Issue, but they failed to convince the other side.

A resolution was presented at the conference regarding the Trinity vs. Oneness debate, and the outcome of the vote wasn't even close. By a margin of 429 to 156, the Trinitarians prevailed in the decision that baptism would be done according to Matthew 28:19. E.N. Bell had made his decision, and he remained with the Assemblies of God.

Having suffered a great defeat, the Oneness advocates walked out of the meeting. About one-third of the Assemblies of God ministers, including Howard Goss, left the AG and set out to form a number of Oneness organizations.

Early Trinitarian ministry of Andrew D. Urshan. Andrew D. Urshan is best known as a pioneer of the Oneness movement, but he got his start in the Trinity. Born in Persia in 1884, Urshan came to the United States in 1902. As a Trinitarian, he received the Holy Ghost with the evidence of speaking in tongues in 1908, and then in 1910, William Durham ordained Urshan as a minister of the Gospel.

Starting in 1913, the "New Issue" began making waves in Trinitarian circles. Urshan however, was not convinced by this new doctrine. He referred to the New Issue as, "The conclusions of men." On page 13 of the April 20, 1918 edition of the Assemblies of God publication, "Weekly Evangel," he defended himself against allegations that he had fallen into the camp of New Issue advocates. Portions of his statement are quoted as follows: "It has been reported lately from this city something that may create a wrong impression that I am supporting the advocators of the "new issue" so-called in our great blessed revival meetings in this city. This is absolutely not so, but rather contrary. I personally believe and stand on the blessed written word of God concerning the great mystery of godliness, not on the conclusions of men, nor in their words of strife concerning God-head teaching, therefore I prayerfully and humbly confess that I believe in one God, the Father, the Son, and the Holy Ghost. Matthew 28:19."

"I believe in Jesus Christ, the Son of the Father, who is the true God and the eternal life. 1 John5:29, 2 John 5."

"I believe that there are three that bear record in heaven the Father, the Word, (Jesus Christ) and the Holy Ghost and these three are one. 1 John 5:7."

"I believe this adorable Three-One God can be only approached and seen in and through the person or face of Jesus Christ the son. 1 Timothy 6:16. Matthew 11:27. John 1:18. John 14:7-11."

During the early years of his ministry, Urshan outright objected to the term, "Oneness." Instead, he referred to "the Trinity in Christ," and he spoke of "the triune God," and he described God as a "Tri-Unity," and he referred to the Godhead as "the Three-One God." Urshan was not bashful when it came to speaking of the "tri-unity," the "three-ness of God," and the "triune being."

During this period of time, many Trinitarians were being re-baptized in the Name of Jesus Christ. Urshan didn't have a problem with people being baptized in Jesus Name, but at the same time, he objected to the idea that it was a *necessity* to be re-baptized in Jesus Name. To him, baptism according to Matthew 28:19 was just as valid as that described in Acts 2:38.

Urshan's belief in the Trinity was so strong that he chose to remain with the Assemblies of God even after a third of the Oneness ministers left the organization in 1916.

Urshan abandons Trinitarianism. After the fourth General Council of the Assemblies of God ratified a strongly-worded statement of faith in 1916, over 150 Oneness ministers withdrew and began organizing a variety of Oneness fellowships. Andrew Urshan however, chose to remain with the Assemblies of God. In spite of his continued fellowship with the AG, he was often accused of harboring notions that were in favor of the New Issue. He was quick to deny those accusations however, by declaring, "This is absolutely not so." Nevertheless, by 1919, Urshan was publishing a good number of overtly Oneness views.

Urshan's writings didn't sit well with the Assemblies of God. They didn't want one of their own leaders to be speaking in favor of the Oneness doctrine, so they had little choice but to address that sticky issue with Urshan before another major disagreement could rise up and split the organization even further. Nevertheless, he continued expressing Oneness views.

In the April 19, 1919 issue of the Christian Evangel, E.N. Bell, chairman of the AG, published an article entitled, "Andrew Urshan's New Stand, a bit of sad news." This article confirmed Urshan's alignment with the New Issue, and broke the news to the readers that he had offered to turn in his AG credentials.

With that, Urshan left the Assemblies of God and began associating with Oneness ministers. Even after defecting from Trinitarianism however, many of the big Oneness names like Haywood, Urshan and Goss still did not consider their Trinitarian brothers to be lost. Not only did they believe that Trinitarians would be saved, they also fellowshipped with them on a frequent basis. Oneness ministers were preaching at Trinitarian events, and Trinitarian ministers were preaching at Oneness events.

There is a very interesting, and often overlooked item of news in that same April 19, 1919 article of the Christian Evangel. R.E. McAlister, the man who had introduced the "New Issue" to the entire world, no longer believed in his own

Oneness message. As Urshan was leaving Trinitarianism and going over to the Oneness camp, R.E. McAlister was leaving the Oneness movement he had created, and was re-joining the Trinitarian movement. Bell's article indicated that after McAlister had seen the errors of the New Issue teaching, he turned against it, and returned to "the old Bible truths."

In explaining what he meant by "errors of the New Issue teaching," Bell quoted directly from Urshan's new Circular (pamphlet). The pamphlet said that the term, "Christ" means, "The Anointed One." Then it said that the Apostle John referred to the Holy Ghost as, the "anointing." Therefore, Jesus Christ is the name of the Holy Ghost. According to Bell, this was flawed logic. *"But the anointing which ye have received of him abideth in you, and ye need not that any man teach you: but as the same anointing teacheth you of all things, and is truth, and is no lie, and even as it hath taught you, ye shall abide in him."* (1 John 2:27)

Does the "anointing" in 1 John 2:27 refer to the Holy Ghost? Notice that the anointing "teacheth you of all things." Then John 14:26 tells us that the Holy Ghost "shall teach you all things." Therefore, according to Oneness teachings, the anointing in 1 John 2:27 refers to the Holy Ghost in John 14:26.

"But the Comforter, which is the Holy Ghost, whom the Father will send in my name, he shall teach you all things, and bring all things to your remembrance, whatsoever I have said unto you." (John 14:26)

However, this linking of "The Anointed One" and the "anointing" was considered by E.N. Bell to be an error. Why? It may be that while "The Anointed One" refers to Christ, the "anointing" may refer to the sanctifying *influence* of the Holy Ghost upon Christians. In other words, the "anointing" is an influence, or a teaching. Bell is trying to tell his readers that Jesus, the Anointed One, is not the same as the anointing, or the influence that Christians receive when they have the Holy Ghost. The term, "The Anointed One," according to Bell, is not interchangeable with the term, the "anointing."

To further understand E.N. Bell's supposition that this play on similar terms was an error, let's look at a couple of other Oneness teachings. Oneness doctrine teaches that Jesus and the Father are one and the same because John 17:22 says, "…that they may be one, even as we are one." *"And the glory which thou gavest me I have given them; that they may be one, even as we are one:"* (John 17:22)

If John 17:22 means that Jesus is the Father because, "…we are one," then the multitude of believers who make up the Church inhabit one physical body as well. Trinitarians would argue that just as individual Christians are not inhabiting one physical body, likewise, Jesus and the Father are not one and the same.

Another Oneness teaching is that Jesus is the Father because John 17:6 says that Jesus manifested his (the Father's) name which he (the Father) had given to him. *"I have manifested thy name unto the men which thou gavest me out of the world: thine they were, and thou gavest them me; and they have kept thy word."* (John 17:6)

Oneness proponents seem to overlook the fact that John 17:12 says that the disciples are also in "His (the Father's) Name." The Oneness argument that John 17:6 proves that Jesus is the Father would necessarily come to the conclusion that the disciples were the Father as well. *"While I was with them in the world, I kept them in thy name: those that thou gavest me I have kept, and none of them is lost, but the son of perdition; that the scripture might be fulfilled."* (John 17:12)

Oneness proponents teach that Jesus is the Father because John 14:10 says that Jesus is in the Father, and the Father is in

Jesus. *"Believest thou not that I am in the Father, and the Father in me? the words that I speak unto you I speak not of myself: but the Father that dwelleth in me, he doeth the works."* (John 14:10)

If this were so, then according to John 14:20, all believers would actually be Jesus, *and* they would be the Father as well. *"At that day ye shall know that I am in my Father, and ye in me, and I in you."* (John 14:20)

Finally, Oneness doctrine teaches that Jesus is the Father because John 10:30 says that he (Jesus) and the Father are one. *"I and my Father are one."* (John 10:30)

The implication of the Oneness interpretation of John 10:30 is that Jesus is saying, "I am the Father." If that were so, then according to John 17:21, all of the disciples were in fact, one physical being because Jesus prayed that they should be one just as he and the Father are one. *"That they all may be one; as thou, Father, art in me, and I in thee, that they also may be one in us: that the world may believe that thou hast sent me."* (John 17:21)

A second "error" pointed out in Bell's article was that according to Urshan, since "Jesus" is the name of the Holy Ghost, then baptism in the Name of Jesus Christ must be the exact Holy Ghost interpretation of Matthew 28:19. Bell argued that since scripture does not provide that same sort of explanation, then this teaching is a "modern invention."

A third "error" pointed out in the article has to do with the New Issue proponents' requirement that people must be re-baptized in Jesus Name in order to be born again. Urshan's pamphlet said, "My message is not against or doing away with our immersion according to Matt. 28:19, but this re-baptism is SOMETHING NEW FROM HEAVEN, given unto many individuals like that of John the Baptist, which he had no special scriptures for."

E.N. Bell said that Urshan was admitting that he had no scripture to back up his claim that Trinitarians must be re-baptized in Jesus Name. Bell emphasized that Urshan was claiming to support "Something New from Heaven." Nowhere in the pamphlet did Urshan make the suggestion that the original Oneness message that went underground after the Nicene Council had finally re-emerged. Instead, Urshan overtly proclaimed that he supported, "Something New from Heaven."

Early Oneness organizations. The Pentecostal Assemblies of the World (PAW) is the oldest Oneness Pentecostal organization in existence. It was loosely founded in 1906 under the leadership of William Seymour, and then in 1912, it was formally organized as a Trinitarian fellowship by D.C.O. Opperman, E.W. Doak, and G.T. Haywood.

Then in 1913, the Pentecostal movement went through a change when hundreds of preachers at a camp meeting in Arroyo Seco listened as Robert. E. McAlister preached that the traditional form of baptism was wrong. He reminded the audience that the Apostles baptized their converts exclusively in the Name of Jesus Christ. Going a step further, he said that not a single person in the Book of Acts was baptized while the titles, Father, Son and Holy Ghost were being invoked.

There were some at the camp meeting who were offended by McAlister's bold remarks. They took McAlister aside and told him not to preach about this "new" baptismal formula theory. However, there were many in the audience who gladly received the new message of Jesus Name baptism. Three of those influenced by this New Issue were Frank Ewart, G.T. Haywood, and Glenn Cook.

Frank Ewart became one of the primary supporters of the New Issue. He taught that the titles, Father, Son, and Holy Ghost, as mentioned in Matthew 28:19, should be summed up as, "Jesus Christ." Further emphasizing his point, he said that the one true God who has revealed himself as the Father, and the Son, and the Holy Spirit is none other than Jesus Christ himself.

In 1914, Ewart re-baptized Glenn Cook, and then Cook re-baptized Ewart. Then, the two boldly announced that anyone baptized in the Triune formula must be re-baptized in the Name of Jesus Christ before they could be regarded as biblically baptized. After this announcement, Ewart and Cook set out to re-baptize multitudes of believers in the Name of Jesus. This action set in motion a doctrinal issue that divided the Pentecostal movement between the Trinitarian doctrine and the Oneness doctrine.

After the emergence of the Oneness doctrine in 1914, a number of Oneness organizations were formed. Some fell by the way side, and others merged, sometimes multiple times. The following list of organizations is not complete by any means, but it includes some of the more influential Oneness organizations.

There were some in the PAW who rejected the New Issue, but there were plenty who were quick to embrace it. Consequently, the Pentecostal Assemblies of the World (PAW) reorganized somewhere around 1914 as a Oneness organization.

G.T. Haywood who was the pastor of one of the largest Pentecostal churches in the world at the time, eagerly accepted the Oneness doctrine and got re-baptized in Jesus Name. Then, he set out to re-baptize his entire congregation. He went on to become the most sought after speaker, teacher and preacher in the Oneness movement.

In 1914, the PAW experienced its first split. There were two basic differences of opinion swirling about within the PAW. As for the Godhead, they were debating among themselves if God is made up of one Person, or if God is made up of three Persons. As for the baptismal formula, they were asking if one should be baptized in the Name of the Father, Son and Holy Ghost, or if one should be baptized in the Name of Jesus.

After about a year of heated debate within the PAW, the Trinitarian believers left the organization. Many of them migrated to the Church of God in Christ (COGIC) before settling within the ranks of the newly-formed Assemblies of God (AG).

In 1915, the remaining Oneness believers in the PAW elected Bishop G. T. Haywood as the organization's first Presiding Bishop. The headquarters of the Pentecostal Assemblies of the World were set up in Portland, Oregon.

After the Fourth General Conference of the Assemblies of God affirmed their stance on the Trinity, Howard Goss left the organization and got involved with the Pentecostal Assemblies of Canada (PAOC).

In January of 1917, a group of Oneness ministers held an organizational meeting in Eureka Springs, Arkansas. When the meeting was over, the new organization was named the General Assembly of the Apostolic Assemblies (GAAA). This organization formed around a number of leading Pentecostal ministers including Howard A. Goss, O.F. Fauss, Frank Ewart, and others. Goss became treasurer of the GAAA.

In 1918, a merger occurred between the Pentecostal Assemblies of the World (PAW) and the General Assembly of Apostolic Assemblies (GAAA). This newly merged organization which was at that time, the only major Oneness

Pentecostal organization, retained the name, Pentecostal Assemblies of the World. They elected G. T. Haywood as their leader. Howard Goss was among the leaders of this newly-merged organization. After the PAW merger, Goss retained the office of treasurer. In 1919, they were joined by Andrew Bar-David Urshan.

In 1919, the Pentecostal Assemblies of the World headquarters were moved from Portland to Indianapolis, and was formally incorporated in the state of Indiana. The incorporators were E. W. Doak, G.T. Haywood, and D.C.O. Opperman.

Then in 1924, a controversy within the ranks of the PAW resulted in a split that occurred mainly along racial lines. After the split, the Pentecostal Assemblies of the World emerged as an organization consisting primarily of black believers. A new Oneness organization, consisting mostly of white believers was formed, and it was named, Pentecostal Ministerial Alliance (PMA). The PMA elected Howard Goss as their General Secretary.

By the year, 1925, three new Oneness organizations had been formed. They were the Apostolic Churches of Jesus Christ

(ACJC), the Pentecostal Ministerial Alliance (PMA), and Emmanuel's Church in Jesus Christ (ECJC).

In 1927, certain ministers felt the need to unify a couple of these organizations. Meeting jointly, the ECJC and the ACJC merged while keeping the name, Apostolic Churches of Jesus Christ. In all, about 400 Oneness Pentecostal ministers participated in this merger.

In 1931, talks commenced between the Apostolic Churches of Jesus Christ (ACJC), and the Pentecostal Assemblies of the World (PAW) regarding a merger. A conference was convened in November, 1931 to work out the details of the merger. Portions of the ACJC name, and portions of the PAW name were utilized in creating the new organization's name. The decided to call themselves the Pentecostal Assemblies of Jesus Christ. At that early stage of the organization, there were also known as the P.A. of J.C. Eventually, it was shortened to PAJC.

The Pentecostal Ministerial Alliance (PMA) found itself poised for some organizational changes in 1932. As a result of this reorganization, the fellowship changed its name to the Pentecostal Church, Incorporated (PCI), and it was determined that Howard Goss would remain as the organization's General Superintendent.

The salvational doctrine of the PCI was simple. Converts were considered saved upon repentance and faith in Christ's atonement for their sins. The convert's sins were remitted at the point of repentance and belief, rather than at baptism. This was in contrast to the position of the Pentecostal Assemblies of Jesus Christ (PAJC) which stated that even though a candidate for conversion had repented, his sins remained with him until water baptism was performed.

The PCI interpreted the term, *"for* the remission of sins" in Acts 2:38 as meaning, *"because of* the remission of sins," instead of, *"in order to obtain* the remission of sins." The position of the leaders of the PCI was that baptism is performed as a public statement that sins had already been remitted. *"Then Peter said unto them, Repent, and be baptized every one of you in the name of Jesus Christ **for** the remission of sins, and ye shall receive the gift of the Holy Ghost."* (Acts 2:38)

As for the Godhead, while the PCI was firmly in the Oneness camp, they still viewed the One God as being triune in nature. This belief allowed them to continue having a relationship with Trinitarian churches and their leaders.

In 1932, Andrew D. Urshan became affiliated with the PAJC. The newly-merged organization was destined for difficulties however, due to racial strife. Because of overt segregation in the South, black ministers would not be welcomed at any conferences that were held below the Mason-Dixon Line. Nevertheless, a conference was held in Tulsa, Oklahoma in 1937, and only the white ministers were allowed to attend.

The 1937 conference was the undoing of many relationships between the white ministers and the blacks. From the black ministers' viewpoint, the whites were thumbing their noses at them. Even though it was decided in Tulsa to hold the next conference in the North where all members could be present, a split was still eminent. In spite of the whites claiming that they had no inclination to segregate themselves from the blacks, it was too late to repair the damage. Many, if not most of the black ministers went back to a revived Pentecostal Assemblies of the World (PAW).

The next PAJC convention (1938) was held in Columbus, Ohio. W.T. Witherspoon was elected to be the General Chairman. Other leaders who took the reins of the mostly white PAJC were A.D. Urshan, O.F. Fauss, Stanley R. Hanby, and S.G. Norris.

United Pentecostal Church. In the 1930's and early 1940's, the Pentecostal Church, Inc. (PCI), and the Pentecostal Assemblies of Jesus Christ (PAJC) were two of the largest Oneness organizations in America. As for the Godhead, these two organizations shared rather compatible viewpoints. The Trinitarians believed that the Father, Son, and Holy Spirit were three distinct Persons, yet they shared the indivisible substance of the one and only God. The Oneness proponents however, declared that the concept of distinct "Persons" in the Godhead logically leads to a belief in three separate gods. The Oneness doctrine claimed that the one God expressed himself in the form of manifestations rather than as distinct Persons.

When it came to the plan of salvation however, the PCI and the PAJC were worlds apart. Most of the membership of the PAJC believed that in order for a prospective convert to be saved, he had to adhere to the command found in Acts 2:38 which states that one should repent, be baptized in the Name of Jesus Christ, and receive the gift of the Holy Ghost with the evidence of speaking in tongues.

The leaders of the PCI were much more sympathetic to the prospect that their Trinitarian brethren could be saved without having to go through the three-step process implied by Acts

2:38. Rather than having to go through the three-step process of repentance, baptism in Jesus Name, and then tarrying for weeks, months or even years for the gift of the Holy Ghost in order to obtain salvation, the Trinitarians trusted in their own dogma that belief in the atonement of the Cross, coupled with accepting Jesus Christ as Lord was sufficient to merit salvation.

In 1936, the PCI and the PAJC entered into discussions regarding a merger, however doctrinal differences forced the two organizations to remain separate for a few more years. Then, just a short time prior to the end of World War II (September 2, 1945), W.T. Witherspoon of the PAJC extended another invitation to the Pentecostal Church, Inc. to explore the possibilities of a merger. At that time, Howard Goss was the General Chairman of the PCI.

In the fall of 1945, both the PAJC and the PCI held their annual conferences in St. Louis. In spite of glaring doctrinal differences regarding the plan of salvation, the two predominantly-white Oneness organizations decided that they had enough common beliefs to unite and form a single denomination. The primary doctrinal stumbling block was the interpretation of Acts 2:38, which happens to be the number one, all important scripture quoted by today's Oneness Pentecostals.

After considerable debate, W.T. Witherspoon sat down at a typewriter and wrote out a statement of compromise which read, "We shall endeavor to keep the unity of the Spirit until we all come into the unity of the faith, at the same time admonishing all brethren that they shall not contend for their different views to the disunity of the body."

By the time the conferences were concluded, the PAJC and the PCI no longer existed. A newly founded organization, called the United Pentecostal Church (UPC), had been formed. Witherspoon's statement had become an integral part of the fundamental doctrine of the newly formed UPC.

The merger of these two Oneness Pentecostal bodies brought together over 1,800 ministers and approximately 900 churches making the UPC the largest of all Oneness organizations. Howard A. Goss, a convert of Charles Parham was elected to be the first General Superintendent of the newly merged organization. Witherspoon had to be content with being the Assistant General Superintendent. One rather interesting point is that Goss, the former leader of the "greasy grace" PCI organization was the person who was elected to lead the newly formed UPC.

In 1972, after feeling the need to be viewed as a world-wide organization, the UPC voted to add the word, "International" to its title. Thereafter, it was known as the United Pentecostal Church International (UPCI).

Here They Come Knocking

Of all the religious organizations listed in this book, two in particular stand out as having a widespread and commonly known reputation of door-to-door evangelism—the Mormons, and Jehovah's Witnesses. Strangely enough, both of these evangelistically-inclined groups have beliefs contrary to those of mainline Christianity. Consequently, it is of benefit to have some knowledge of what they believe before agreeing to sit down and talk with them.

Mormons. In addition to the Bible, Mormons, otherwise known as the Latter Day Saints, believe the Book of Mormon to be Inspired Scripture. According to their beliefs, the angel Moroni directed Joseph Smith to a buried stone box containing a set of golden plates which were engraved with hieroglyphics. Once translated to English, the contents of the golden plates became known as the Book of Mormon, and it described an ancient American civilization.

The Mormons believe Jesus to be the eldest of God's children, and he conquered sin and death so that God's other children could return. Every person who lives on earth will be resurrected, and nearly all of them will be received into various kingdoms of glory. To be accepted into the highest kingdom however, a person must fully accept Christ through faith, repentance, and through ordinances such as baptism and the laying on of hands.

Mormons believe the Father, Son, and Holy Ghost are three distinct beings, and the Father and Jesus have glorified, physical bodies—while the Holy Ghost is a spirit without a physical body. They also believe there are other gods and goddesses outside the Godhead, such as a Heavenly Mother—who is the wife of God the Father—and that faithful Latter-day Saints may attain their own godhood in the afterlife.

Jehovah's Witnesses. This group believes there is no hell or fiery torment. They believe 144,000 selected humans will go to Heaven, but the majority will be resurrected to a cleansed earth after Armageddon. Jehovah's Witnesses consider all other present-day religions to be false, and they will be destroyed.

Jehovah's Witnesses believe Jesus Christ began to rule in Heaven as king of God's kingdom in October 1914, and that Satan was subsequently ousted from heaven to earth, resulting in "woe" to humanity. They believe Jesus' presence includes an unknown period beginning with his inauguration as king in Heaven in 1914, and ending when he comes to bring a final judgment against humans on earth.

Jehovah's Witnesses believe that only Jehovah's Witnesses represent true Christianity, and that other religions fail to meet all the requirements set by God and will soon be destroyed. Jehovah's Witnesses are taught that it is vital to remain separate from the world. The Witnesses' literature defines the world as the mass of mankind apart from Jehovah's approved servants, and teach that it is morally contaminated and ruled by Satan. Witnesses are taught that association with worldly people presents a danger to their faith, and are instructed to minimize social contact with non-members to better maintain their own standards of morality. Attending a university is discouraged and trade schools are suggested as an alternative.

www.ingramcontent.com/pod-product-compliance
Lightning Source LLC
Chambersburg PA
CBHW061426160726
47995CB00003B/766